December 2020

Because you & a
have integrity, a
steady moral compass,
you will make an
excellent attorney.
So proud of you!
I love you,
Mom

DOESN'T HURT TO ASK

DOESN'T HURT TO ASK

USING THE POWER OF QUESTIONS
TO COMMUNICATE, CONNECT,
AND PERSUADE

TREY GOWDY

CROWN
FORUM

NEW YORK

Published in the United States by Crown Forum,
an imprint of Random House, a division of
Penguin Random House LLC, New York.

CROWN FORUM with colophon is a registered trademark of
Penguin Random House LLC.

LIBRARY OF CONGRESS CATALOGING-IN-PUBLICATION DATA
Names: Gowdy, Trey, author.
Title: Doesn't hurt to ask / Trey Gowdy.
Description: First edition. | New York: Crown Forum, [2020]
Identifiers: LCCN 2020007613 (print) |
LCCN 2020007614 (ebook) | ISBN 9780593138915 (Hardback) |
ISBN 9780593138922 (Ebook)
Subjects: LCSH: Persuasion (Psychology) |
Interpersonal communication.
Classification: LCC BF637.P4 G68 2020 (print) |
LCC BF637.P4 (ebook) | DDC 153.8/52—dc23
LC record available at https://lccn.loc.gov/2020007613
LC ebook record available at https://lccn.loc.gov/2020007614

Printed in the United States of America on acid-free paper

crownforum.com

6   8   9   7   5

First Edition

To Terri; our children, Watson and Abigail;
and my parents, Hal and Novalene Gowdy

CONTENTS

FROM COURTROOM TO CONGRESS

WHY I PERSUADE

For sixteen years, I stood in front of countless groups of twelve people who were unsuccessful in getting out of jury duty. (Okay, maybe that isn't fair. But admit it! You are hardly enthused when you get a summons in the mail.) However, in my experience, despite their hesitation most people wind up either enjoying their jury service or, at a minimum, appreciating the majesty of our justice system. The courthouse reflects real life, with all the pain and joy, the justice and injustice, and the raw emotions that come from trying to harness and adjudicate human nature. Your life most likely doesn't involve a courthouse, but the "trials" are just as real. Those "trials" could be in business settings, community meetings, schools, or at home.

After nearly a hundred jury trials in both federal and state court—ranging in cases from firearms violations to narcotics trafficking, kidnappings to carjackings, sexual assault to robbery, child abuse to murder—the courtroom has become the single most peaceful and comfortable place for me. I love the logic. I love the rules. I love the strategy. I love the need for quick thinking. I love the opportunity to seek truth. I love the entire human spectrum epitomized by people and procedures. But mostly, I love the courtroom because I love the art of persuasion, and I've dedicated myself to being as good at it as I possibly can be.

I owe that to my mother. She did a lot of things workwise while I was growing up with my three sisters, but the job she enjoyed the most was being a victim advocate for the local solicitor's office. Victim advocates advise the victims of crimes and their families on what their rights are as victims and demystify the criminal process. If needed or requested, victim advocates sit with the victim and their families through trials, pleas, and sentencing hearings.

When I was home during the summers in college and law school, my mom would come in after work frustrated about our criminal justice system. She would openly wonder, "Why does a defendant, someone charged with a crime, get to hire any lawyer he or she wants, but the victim cannot? The victim is stuck with the prosecutor assigned to the case. Why can't a victim go hire the best lawyer too?"

That's a good question, Mom. I know the textbook answer—the crime is really against the state, not against an individual—but textbook answers are of no solace to a victim being cross-examined by a skilled criminal defense attorney, while the perpetrator may or may not be cross-examined by a skilled prosecutor. You were right, Mom. Victims are entitled to a good lawyer. Victims are entitled to a lawyer who can set the stage with the right expectations in an opening statement. Victims are entitled to a lawyer who can connect with a jury both verbally and nonverbally. Victims are entitled to a lawyer who can use direct questions to skillfully elicit the testimony in a compelling, logical way. They are entitled to a lawyer who can cross-examine defendants effectively without looking down at their notes. They are entitled to a lawyer who can marry passion with reason in a closing argument and move a jury to consensus, even overcoming the highest evidentiary burden our culture recognizes, which is beyond a reasonable doubt. They are entitled to a lawyer who can anticipate what the defense attorney is going to do before they do it and have a plan to combat it. They are entitled to someone who knows the ins and outs of persuasion.

Even outside of a courtroom setting, people want to be both effectively advocated for and effective advocates themselves. If there is a conversation at work about a promotion or a new line of business, you will want to be part of that conversation, and being part of that conversation may very well be in direct proportion to your effectiveness as a communicator. In fact, you want to be considered an indispensable part of that conversation.

That is what I strove to be for those sixteen years in the courtroom—an advocate the victim would have picked if he or she could do what my mom wanted them to be able to do: pick any lawyer in the country to be their lawyer. The weight of being an effective advocate for a victim or a victim's family was heavy. But that weight is no lighter in other realms of your own life. You too will need to successfully advocate about something or someone. You will need to persuade others to either come closer to your way of thinking on an issue or at least see why it is you believe what you believe. The courtroom was my job site but you have your own job site, and the need to competently process and communicate information toward a desired outcome is every bit as essential on your job site as it was on mine. The skill set needed is the same whether the issue is murder, marketing, or motherhood.

I sometimes refer to "receiving line" jobs. Those are the

jobs you want people to remember you for when you are gone. I've asked my wife to do two things if I die before she does: (1) wait until after my funeral to start dating, and (2) make sure our children remember that their father loved being a prosecutor more than any other job. It's the job I want to be remembered for, because it was the job with the most meaning, the highest sense of purpose, and the most challenging objective: to persuade within the rules of fairness and due process and to move the jury from not guilty to guilty using credibility, facts, reasoning, passion, logic, and an entire mosaic of words.

You will have your own version of how this conversation will go as it relates to your own life—but it is never too soon to think about how you want to impact the world in which you live, work, and love.

There is one more thing I hope my wife remembers:

(3) Make sure those friends and family closest to us remember the last case I prosecuted and why I did it.

If you ever visited my office in Washington, DC, and wondered who the little girl was in the picture beside my family's picture, she was the last victim in the last criminal case I will ever try. She was the reason I stood in front of a jury one final time.

Meah Weidner was a beautiful ten-year-old girl born with cerebral palsy. She was beaten and shaken to death by her mother's boyfriend. The boyfriend was a firefighter and an EMT with no criminal record. He said her injuries were caused when she fell out of her wheelchair while having a seizure, and he claimed that he may have accidentally hurt her attempting CPR to save her life. But it was an accident, he contended, not a crime.

I had one foot out of the door. I was already on my way to Congress. Swearing in was just a few weeks away. Surely someone else in the office could take this case. There were plenty of very good prosecutors in our office and someone else could do a good job for Meah. But I could not get my mother's voice out of my head: "Why is it a defendant can hire the best lawyer money can buy, but the victim cannot?"

It was a combination of my mother's voice and what father-hood does to a person that prompted me to take the file and take the case for myself. For the little girl who could no longer talk, I would talk. For the girl who couldn't defend herself, I would defend her. For the girl confined to a wheelchair, I would pace back and forth in front of the jury, assigning the same value to her life that they would to their own children. I would persuade effectively on her behalf because it was just and it was right.

It was a tough case convincing twelve people that a man with a good job and no criminal history could kill a defenseless child. But that is what happened. And I used logic, facts, and—most important—questions to do it.

I asked questions of the jury. Sure, some were questions to get them the knowledge they needed to form an educated opinion. Some were questions that they and I already knew the answer to. But all questions were so that they could arrive at the truth of their own accord.

Eventually, all twelve said "Guilty." They convicted the man of killing Meah Weidner, and the judge sentenced him to life without the possibility of parole. It was clear by the tone of the room and the speed with which the jury reached a verdict that they were moved by this young girl's life. *Moved* to feel what I felt. *Moved* to assign the same value to Meah's life they would assign to their own child's or their own grandchild's. *Moved* to do the right thing.

Meah's picture on my desk was a reminder of many things: the fragility of life, the innocence of the young, the power of standing up for others, and the need within each of us to advocate for something significant. And while using questions to move others is admittedly a unique way of persuading, I am convinced it is an indispensable part of persuasion at the highest level. Most people can attempt to persuade by saying what they believe and why, but can you persuade by asking the right questions, at the right time, in the right order? More important, can you, in essence, have the person with whom you are talking convince themselves?

You do not need to be in a courtroom to advocate for others. You do not need to be in Congress to champion a cause. Opportunities to persuade abound. From the courtroom to the living room, from across the aisle to across the desk talking to a client, from convincing a jury to convincing your boss, each of us has opportunities, and occasionally obligations, to persuade.

The most effective persuaders listen as much as they talk. The most effective persuaders ask as many questions as they answer. Asking questions is more than a grudging prerequisite to gaining information. Asking questions, in the right way and at the right time, may well prove to be the most effective tool you have when it comes to moving someone closer to understanding your position or simply moving others closer to one another.

MAYBE CONGRESS? MAYBE NOT.

Those sixteen years as a prosecuting attorney taught me how to be a lawyer. They also taught me about my fellow citizens and how to communicate with them, persuade them, and cajole them with positive proof, and how to deconstruct unreliable evidence. The courtroom is a kind of cultural and anthropological petri dish where all sides of the human spectrum are tested, analyzed, and tried. Which is why what works in a courtroom is precisely what works in real life.

If you use the processes and procedures employed in our justice system in your living room or conference room, someone is likely to state the obvious: "This isn't a courtroom." The late Elijah Cummings, who was a phenomenal lawyer before his distinguished career in Congress, once gently chided me during a committee hearing, "Is this a courtroom? . . . Are we using the Federal Rules of Evidence here?" Former IRS Commissioner John Koskinen, with whom I always had a pleasant relationship outside of the committee conference room, once answered a question by asking, "Is this a trial, is someone on trial here?" No. Committee hearings are not courtrooms, and they do not follow courtroom rules on evidence, procedure, or process. But maybe they should. The policies, precepts, procedures, and rules employed in our justice system are not inherently "right" simply because we use them in a courtroom. Those policies, precepts, procedures, and rules are used in courtrooms because they have stood the test of time, and we collectively accept them as being the best tools for elucidating the truth. In other words, something isn't right because we use it in a courtroom—we use it in a courtroom because it is right. The rightness is what came first.

Even though I loved justice, fairness, pursuing truth, and persuading juries, I left the courtroom because I could not answer my own questions about what happened *outside* the courtroom. I could not reconcile my spiritual beliefs with what I was witnessing daily. Man was consistently and increasingly inhumane toward his fellow man. Innocents suffered. People killed those they claimed to love. The vulnerable were victimized. There was gratuitous violence, depravity, and malice.

In the real world, the vast majority of people are good, kind, law abiding, and willing to help others. But in the justice system that is not what you see, and eventually you get the population's proportions misaligned. There are no trials for good, decent, or kind people in the courtroom. The trials are for those who murder, rape, and commit burglaries. When you're interacting with these types on a day-to-day basis, you quickly acquire a disjointed view of mankind. When evil is all you see, you fall prey to believing it is all that exists.

I remember that my growing skepticism was often met with the ol' Christian adage (and loose biblical reference) "All things work together for good." When you grow up in the buckle of the Bible Belt, you hear that phrase a lot.

All things, huh? What about the children who had cigarettes extinguished on their faces? The children who were sexually assaulted? The innocent couple beaten to death with a hammer? The three-month-old sewn back together because her father raped her? What about Meah? Is that what you mean by "all things work together for good"?

I was pretty good in a courtroom. I could convince twelve people beyond a reasonable doubt almost anytime I wanted and needed to convince them. For sixteen years, I could get twelve complete strangers to come together and reach unanimity. Persuading my fellow citizens or judges was never the hard part for me.

What was hard was the drive home from the courtroom each evening after work where the answers began to be outpaced by the questions. At the end of the day, watching the daylight lose its battle with darkness, I struggled to unsee the images from crime scene photos. Lying awake in bed while my family was fast asleep, I struggled to separate the sound of the wind outside from the sound of evil and depravity trying to come inside. I was having a very hard time separating work from the rest of life. And so too were the people most precious to me. For almost a year our daughter would drag her pillow and blanket into our bedroom and put them on the floor beside our bed. On the floor on *my* side of the bed, of course. She knew her mom would make her go back to her room. She knew her father would not. I even tried working it out with God, but the God I was brought up to talk to in times of disquiet or angst was either not listening or not talking back.

It wasn't the defense attorney or the jury in the courtroom that defeated me. It was the lawyer and the jury in my own head.

I could never persuade myself that a loving God would allow a child to be burned to death, beaten to death, or raped by her own father. I could never persuade myself that a loving God would allow a child with cerebral palsy to be killed by her mother's boyfriend. I could never persuade myself all things were going to work for good in the end because the end for many innocent people was death— and there is no bargaining, compromising, or persuading death. For those who survived, it was a lifetime of pain, fear, and distrust; their questions were always better than my answers. I could tell them the *who;* I just could never adequately tell them the *why.*

So I left the courtroom with just the tiniest remnant of faith left. I left as a cynic with just the slightest flicker of light. I left before the questions turned to anger and the anger turned to full-fledged cynicism. Barely.

Now what? Where does someone who loves to persuade turn when the courtroom is no longer an option? Maybe an even bigger jury pool? Maybe politics? Maybe Congress?

Maybe not.

Oddly enough, I did leave Congress with a higher opinion of mankind than when I left the courtroom, but I left nevertheless. I left the courtroom because the questions were better than the answers. I left Congress because the questions never matter in politics. Almost everyone in Washington, DC, already has his or her mind made up.

Even outside of Washington, DC, almost everyone has his or her mind made up on the issues. Politics is nonstop. Every day is a miniature Election Day. More and more facets of life seem to have political undertones. NFL games are politicized. Music and movie award shows involve politics. Hurricanes and viruses have political undertones. Even at our own kitchen tables, politics is lurking, trying to insert itself.

I do not recall a single person's mind ever being changed during a committee or floor debate during the eight years I was in Congress. Persuasion requires an open mind, and you cannot move someone who is unwilling to move. You cannot persuade someone who is unwilling to be persuaded. Jurors are, by definition, willing to be persuaded. Members of Congress, at least in the modern political environment, either cannot be persuaded or cannot admit they were.

After eight years of Congress, I became convinced the questions were irrelevant, because there was little opportunity to persuade anyone other than myself. It was wildly inefficient but surprisingly informative. While I was in Congress, strangely, I became more open to being persuaded. It wasn't floor speeches or committee hearings. It was being exposed to smart, credible people, with fact-centric arguments who were making an effort to be heard, understood, and willing to hear and understand me in the process.

My time in DC led me to understand that people are arriving to the table with different sets of experiences and that everyone's opinions are filtered through the lens of those experiences. Whether I agree or disagree doesn't matter. Everyone deserves to have a seat at the table and if everyone arrives to the table with the same tools and knowledge to successfully persuade, arguments turn to dialogue, and dialogue turns to earnest questions, and questions turn to real and meaningful influence.

It was on the marbled floors of the Capitol that I realized persuasion is not about winning arguments—it's about effectively and efficiently advocating for what it is you believe to be true. Persuasion is a far more subtle methodology whereby, when the person is asked the right set of questions, they will arrive at the point you are trying to make of their own accord. Persuasion is about understanding what people believe and why they believe it and using that to either debunk or confirm their position. Persuasion is subtle, incremental, and deliberate. It has the potential to be life changing.

WANT TO START?

In July 1986, I was at the beach with my childhood best friend, Keith Cox, and his family. It was the summer after I graduated from college and I had no idea what I was going to do next— a history major with no direction and no motivation. My lack of a plan for the rest of my life was exceeded only by a lack of a desire to have a plan for the rest of my life. As the family and I sat out on the porch one morning, overlooking the Atlantic Ocean, Keith's mother asked me to stay with her while she finished her cup of coffee. Everyone else had left for the beach.

"What are you going to do next, honey?" she asked.

"I don't know, Mrs. Cox, maybe go to Las Cruces, New Mexico, and do construction work with a college buddy." We sat and talked and she gently asked me question after question after question. So. Many. Questions. But all of them out of the love a mom has for her son's best friend and a kid she had known most of his life. She did not try to talk me into anything. She was not a psychiatrist or a lawyer. She was a stay-at-home mom who cared enough to ask the right questions in the right order.

What she accomplished in those thirty minutes changed my life. She took me from doing construction in Las Cruces, New Mexico, to going to law school. By listening, caring, asking the right follow-up questions, and having her objective in sight before she ever asked me to stay behind that morning, she managed to conquer my self-doubt and appeal to a source of pride at the same time. She said, "Surprise the skeptics, Trey, and do something amazing in life. Just know it will not surprise me because I've seen it in you since you were a child. It will be our secret. Just go surprise everyone else!"

Getting someone to do something they were not planning on doing. Convincing someone to buy into something they never knew they were looking for. *That* is persuasion. Someone else's mom took me from building houses half a country away to studying torts and constitutional law in South Carolina. It took her thirty minutes. Armed with compassion, a predetermined outcome in mind, and the right questions, she persuaded me to do more than just go to school for three more years. She didn't care whether I went to law school or not. What she cared about was me; and that I left for the beach that morning persuaded to have higher expectations for myself than what I woke up with that morning.

You may never find yourself in front of a jury in a criminal prosecution arguing for a particular verdict, or offering yourself for elected office in a political campaign. You simply want to be heard. You just want to be understood. You want to effectively communicate what you believe, why you believe it, and why perhaps others should adopt your position as well. Maybe you will never be in a highly charged debate for a seat in the United States Senate. Maybe it will be something much more important than that—like convincing a child to aspire higher, expect more, compete harder. Maybe you just want to be able to effectively express your position to a co-worker, a family member, or a spouse. Maybe you want to speak up but are not sure you are well enough equipped to engage in the banter at your place of business, worship center, or class reunion.

I want to help you become a better advocate and become

better at advancing what you believe through the art of asking the right questions, at the right time, in the right order, and in the right form—regardless, in some instances, of whether you know the answer to your own questions or not. Persuasion is in part an affirmative duty to prove, but it is also in part proving your point through the art of questioning.

You want to start?

You must at the outset answer the most fundamental question of all. It is my favorite question to ask because it's self-directed. I asked it of police officers and lay witnesses as a prosecutor. I asked it of myself before every congressional hearing. I currently ask it of myself before any speech, whether it is to a roomful of attorneys or my wife's first-grade students.

What do you want to accomplish?

And the first cousins to that question follow closely behind:

What is your objective?

How do you measure success at the end of the interaction?

Who is your jury?

How hard will it be to prove it?

Whether you are trying to convince a jury to convict a defendant of a potentially capital crime or convince your teenager to clean up his or her room, before you begin your interaction—before you ever open your mouth—these are the questions to ask yourself. Admittedly, convincing the teenager to clean his or her room is the tougher case, but it is also the one you are much more likely to see on a daily basis.

There are times when what you want is less affirmative. Sometimes you desire to move your listener to your side of the ideological spectrum. Maybe it's not about your teenager cleaning his room, but about convincing him to make certain choices regarding his college major. Rather than seeking to make a point ("Vote for my beliefs because they're right!") or prove a proposition ("You know, son, English majors are way more likely to be adaptable candidates in the job force"), you have to move them gently to a specific objective in mind. Maybe it's not to win a vote for your candidate, but rather for that person to *not* vote for *their* candidate. There were times in Congress when my objective was not to get someone to vote with me (because I knew that was never going to happen), but rather my objective was to get them to vote for a lesser form of what they wanted or take a coffee break and miss the committee vote altogether (kidding . . . kind of). For my son, Watson, it was less about my wanting him to study English and more about his *not* studying his first choice: political science. Since no teenager—or anyone for that matter—likes being told directly what to do, asking questions becomes the subtlest and most effective way to persuade. He wanted political science. I wanted English. He chose philosophy in the end, so I think I won.

Regardless of whom you are talking to and regardless of who your jury is, you must have full command of your objective before you open your mouth.

Are you trying to begin a relationship, repair one, enhance one, or end one?

Are you trying to pacify or infuriate?

Is your objective consensus or conflict?

If your objective is to fracture a relationship, infuriate an audience, ratify a deeply held albeit wrong conviction in others, this book will not offer you much aid. For most of my interactions with other individuals or groups, the objective is to either gently move the listener to a new position or gain a renewed enthusiasm for an old one.

So how do you persuade? What works? What does not work?

We are going to explore in this book how to persuade, why it is the most worthwhile skill set to adopt, and all the tools you can equip yourself with to become persuasive on the issues that matter in your life and with the people who matter in your life.

In Part 1, we'll focus on the self-directed questions and we'll lay the groundwork on the essentials: Why questions? What is persuasion really? I'll help you land on your objective, know your jury, and establish your burden of proof as well as walk you through what does and doesn't work when it comes to being a good communicator.

Once you know those factors you can begin the act of persuasion. In Part 2, the self-directed questions pivot and become directed at the *persuadee*. Here we'll focus on specific types of questions you can use as well as tools to help formulate your questions. There are times the questions are earnest—really trying to get information. Sometimes you want to pose questions strategically to get the answer you want, and other times, the answer doesn't really matter and it is instead to elicit a reaction—to debunk and impeach your "jury."

Part 3 shows you how to put the art of persuasion into action in your day-to-day life. While I may be a cynic, much of persuasion is about idealism. It's about open-minded people who can have meaningful dialogue about what it is they truly care about. About people on both sides of the aisle who really listen and are open to being persuaded.

Of course, when we are impassioned by certain things we believe in, we can feel called to proselytize on their behalf and we pull out all the calculated stops to do so. But persuasion is doing this in a constructive way. The art of asking the right question, in the right form, and at the right time is an essential arrow in your quiver of communication. In fact, the ability to ask the right questions, listen to the response, and follow up in a systematic way is essential if you want to move the hearts and minds of those you are speaking to.

And that should be our objective in persuasion: striving to communicate and to *move* those with whom we are interacting. To *move* someone from a yes to a no. To *move* someone to a maybe. To *move* someone to see our side. To *move* someone to get a new angle and new perspective. To *move* them to feel what you feel, to see what you see, to think what you think. *Move* them to do what's worthy, what's good, and what's right. *Move* them to hire you, to give you a chance, to give you more responsibility. *Move* someone to take a chance on your idea. *Move* someone to invest as much in what you are trying to do as you have invested.

Now let's get moving.

PART 1

WHAT YOU NEED TO KNOW BEFORE YOU OPEN YOUR MOUTH

THERE IS SUCH A THING AS A STUPID QUESTION

WHAT COLOR WAS THE BLUE BAG?

Murder cases are somber events. One life has already been lost. Another person is on trial facing the real prospect of life in prison without the possibility of parole—or even more solemn—the possibility of receiving the death penalty. So, as you can imagine, there is no place for humor in any criminal trial. And yet, in my first death penalty trial I had the whole room in tears of laughter. Whoever said "There is no such thing as a stupid question" was not sitting in the Spartanburg County Courthouse in the fall of 2001.

In this case, a convenience store clerk was robbed and killed over a meaninglessly small amount of money. The clerk was a hardworking, good, and decent man who overcame a lot in life and who would have given the suspect the money had he just asked for it.

In most of these cases, there are but two witnesses and one (the victim) is dead, so you are reliant on the defendant's affirmative statements, confessions, or false exculpatory statements in addition to forensics or whatever physical evidence you may have. But in this case, there was another witness. He was sitting off to the side playing a video poker game when the robbery and shooting took place.

Whenever you have an additional witness, you want to meet with them ahead of time to get a sense of what they are going to say and how to prepare for it. In this case, I met with this witness many times. He was vitally important—singularly important in fact—and while he was likely to be nervous testifying in a death penalty trial, he was earnest and credible.

The time came for him to take the stand. It's important to set the scene for the jury: the dimensions of the store, where this witness was sitting relative to the cash register and the clerk, his opportunity to observe, the absence of drugs or alcohol impacting his ability to perceive, and every other question you can anticipate the jury might have.

"Was anything between you and the front door of the store?"

"No, sir."

"Was anything obstructing your view?"

"No, sir."

"Were the lights on?"

"Yes, sir."

"Was the room smoky or cloudy?"

"No, sir."

"Were you under the influence of alcohol?

"No, sir."

"Pardon the personal nature of the question, but were you under the influence of any drugs prescribed or otherwise?"

"No, sir."

"Did you notice the suspect when he walked through the front door?"

"Yes, sir."

"Was anyone else present in the store when the suspect walked in?"

"Just me and the clerk."

"Did you take your eyes off the suspect when he walked in?"

"No, sir."

"Did you have a clear view of the suspect?"

"Yes, sir."

"What happened next?"

"Well, the man walked to the clerk at the counter and pulled out a gun."

"Could you see the gun?"

"Yes, sir."

"Can you describe the gun for the jury?"

"Yes, sir. It was black and looked like a pistol, not a re-volver."

This witness was doing great. He was under control. Clear. Precise. But, apparently, I could not stand prosperity because I had to keep going.

"Sir, I notice you are not wearing glasses. Were you wearing glasses that night?"

"No, sir."

"Is your vision good?"

"Yes, sir. I have perfect vision in my right eye."

What did he just say? Umm, Mr. Witness, you are not a Cyclops! You have two eyes, I thought to myself.

What have I gotten myself into? How do I extricate myself from this? What in the world do I ask or say next? Do I let it go and hope the jury didn't hear him? Or hope the jury doesn't recall that all humans have two eyes? You have to do something, idiot Trey, you can't just leave it hanging like that.

"Of course you do, Mr. Witness, of course you do," was all I could come up with.

"And your left eye . . . is . . . ?"

(Painful silence.)

"It's fake, sir."

"Well, of course it is, Mr. Witness. It's prosthetic."

"No, sir . . . it's fake," he said.

I have one eyewitness and am just now learning—along with everyone else—that he is a one-eyed witness.

I was rattled. I was wishing I was literally anywhere else in the world. Château d'If? Sign me up. Anywhere else other than in that courtroom having not asked this witness about his eye(s) before we got to court.

It can't get any worse than this, right? Except it always can, and in this case, it did.

"What happened next?" I asked.

"Well, the suspect had a blue bag in his hand."

"Okay, what color was the blue bag?"

Laughter exploded throughout the courtroom and that one eye was looking at me like I had lost my mind.

Maybe he didn't hear me so I repeated the question again. "Sir, what color was the blue bag?"

More laughter.

What is going on? Why are people laughing in a death penalty trial? Before I could ask the dumbest question in the history of the English-speaking world a third time, the judge took mercy and said, "Mr. District Attorney, I think the jury knows what color the blue bag was now! You can move on."

Questions can be affirmative. Questions can be a genuine desire for more information. Questions can be corroborative. You already know the answer, but someone else in your "jury" does not, so you use questions to impart information to others, rather than yourself. Questions can be impeaching or undercutting. Questions can be defensive. They can allow you to regroup, deflect, redirect someone's attention so you can live to fight another moment or another day.

And then there are just plain stupid questions.

There are good questions and bad questions and sometimes the same question can be either depending on the circumstances in which it is asked. Asking my eyewitness about his vision was a fantastic question to ask . . . in my office weeks before trial.

There is a picture my staff at the Solicitor's Office* gave me from this trial. It was taken by a local newspaper photographer snapped at precisely the moment this witness said "I have perfect vision in my right eye." My staff gave me the picture from that trial because there was absolutely no discernible reaction on my face when the witness referenced his one eye. Inside I was dying. Outside the jury saw nothing—that is, until I compounded that error by asking what color the blue bag was. I survived the first bad question only to squander the moment by asking the second.

DEFENSE MECHANISM

No one is born knowing how to ask the right questions. Even the brightest among us is not necessarily good at asking questions. The art of doing so can flow from any number of impetuses. For me, it was the convergence of several rivers of thought. It was equal parts (1) a lack of confidence in my own abilities, (2) an acknowledgment of what human nature is at its core—that people like to talk more than they like to listen,

---

* South Carolina calls district attorneys by a different name: circuit solicitors. The job description is the same. Solicitors prosecute all criminal cases in a jurisdiction.

(3) many hours spent in endless inner dialogue, and (4) an awareness that asking the right question is a devilish way to turn the tables.

The chief motivation for using questions rather than declarative statements was and remains impetus number one—that it is a defense mechanism for me. I never thought I was smart enough to participate in conversations with smart people, but I was drawn to be around them.

My dad was smart. He was a medical doctor. So I would ask him questions about medicine. What does the top number mean for blood pressure? Why is 95 a high resting heart rate? How do children get leukemia?

My best friend growing up, Keith Cox, wound up going to Duke University and became an oral surgeon—he was *really* smart. Do I let him know I am not, or do I mask it by asking questions?

Judge Randy Bell was one of the smartest people I met in my life. He was a judge on the South Carolina Court of Appeals. He ultimately was elected to the South Carolina Supreme Court but died before he could take office.

I met him when he was at the Court of Appeals in my first year out of law school. He was a dialysis patient and had to travel from Columbia, South Carolina, to Augusta, Georgia, for dialysis and he needed someone to drive him. So I did. He was a legal scholar. He was an expert on Roman culture. He knew the English common law and could lead the discussion on natural law versus positivism. It is human nature to want to impress someone like Randy Bell—to talk about what I knew and to participate in conversation. I remember driving him to Augusta one afternoon early in our relationship. He was talking about the Nuremberg Trials, something I then knew nothing about. He then moved to contributory negligence versus comparative negligence, something else I knew nothing about. He moved from topic to topic—from Roman mythology to deontology—trying to find something, anything, to which I could possibly contribute.

He failed.

So finally he asked, "Well, son, what *do* you know something about? What would you like to talk about?"

Mainly I wanted to talk about how in the heck I found myself in the car with an expert on Roman law but I said, "NASCAR, I've really gotten into NASCAR lately."

"Great," he responded. "Tell me about the origins of NASCAR."

Silence.

"I know I like Richard Petty. That's about all I know, Your Honor."

That was another low point for me. Armed with an undergraduate degree in history and a law degree but devoid of any real knowledge of either, I was in a car with a soon to be justice of the South Carolina Supreme Court, and he was desperately trying, without any success, to find any topic in the universe I knew enough about to fill a car ride from Columbia, South Carolina, to Augusta, Georgia, and back. I had the same recurring sinking feeling of inadequacy: *I just don't feel very smart. How do I mask it? How do I cover it up? How do I participate in conversations or in professional interactions without revealing these massive gaps in knowledge?*

You can either get smart quickly or find a way to fully conceal your perceived lack of knowledge. You can fill the gaps or you can fill the time. Or maybe, just maybe, you can find a way to fill both simultaneously—by asking questions.

No, I don't know anything about Roman mythology, but I remember a little about Greek mythology. Are the gods different or do the same gods just have different names? Who is your favorite god? Which godlike power would you want if you could pick, Judge Bell? You seem more of a fan of Rome than Athens; how did that come about? What can you tell me about Spartan culture? Was my hometown of Spartanburg named for Sparta?

English common law? Don't know much about that. But I do know enough to ask why some common law is codified or passed by legislative bodies and some not? If there is a conflict between common law and statutory law, which prevails? Is there any federal common law, Judge Bell?

You can learn and pass the time by taking advantage of one of the greatest human needs we have: the desire to be heard. Most people are wired to want to talk, so I take advantage of that. People want to talk more than they want to listen, and if I can leverage human nature I can mask my own deficiencies. So I suppress or subrogate my own desire to be heard and replace it with my desire to avoid being perceived as uneducated—isn't that a win for both of us? You get to talk, I get to listen and learn, and I avoid that sinking feeling of not measuring up. Trust me, asking questions is always your *safest* bet.

STUPID QUESTIONS ARE BETTER THAN STUPID ANSWERS

When it comes to the art of persuasion, we have typically been led to think of the following format: opening statement, make a point, state an argument. Then there's a long stream of declarations, statements, affirmations, presentations, proclamations, pronunciations to slowly build an argument with as few holes as possible and as many powerful assertions as one can fit in a breath. That's the traditional model. But what if there is a better way?

Rarely do we think of persuasion as asking a series of questions. Questions are considered reactive more than proactive, right? Questions are sometimes seen as evidence you don't know the answer to something. Questions can make you seem weak, ill-informed, unknowing, and uncertain in your beliefs. That may be what others would have us believe, but it is diametrically opposed to my own experience. Questions can gather the time, the information, and the interpersonal connectivity to persuade in ways that simply proclaiming what you believe cannot accomplish.

We've already witnessed that the old adage "There is no such thing as a stupid question" was easily and swiftly proven wrong in my case, but there is some truth worth acknowledging there. There are ill-thought-out, poorly phrased, and unwise questions, to be sure, but even the most stupid question is a thousand times better than a stupid declarative statement.

You own every declarative comment that comes out of your mouth, but with questions you have an out. Because of that, questions are perhaps first and foremost the safest route in the art of persuasion.

No matter what you ask, you can say "I didn't know—that's why I asked" if you were dead wrong. You can say "I thought so," if in fact you are right. You are guilty of nothing except seeking more information. It's the difference between sounding stupid and being stupid.

Sounding stupid might be: Who's the author of *Crime and Punishment*?

Being stupid is: Leo Tolstoy is the author of *Crime and Punishment*.

The first shows a lack of information, sure, but the second shows that you think you know something that in reality you don't. It discredits everything that comes out of your mouth from that moment on. The first can be an honest lapse in memory. The second is a dishonest lapse in intelligence.

Who would you trust down the line, the guy who is honest and asks fair questions or the guy who says things that are obviously not true? The guy who's inquisitive or the guy who lies with conviction? We've all seen the guy in a business meeting who has made a false statement in hopes of bolstering a point or making the sale, only to be caught in his lie instantaneously or down the road. The minute you make a false declarative, you lose credibility with the person with whom you are talking or whoever might be listening.

And while we will most certainly dive into this more, there are *less* stupid questions to ask that accomplish all the best reasons for pursuing the art of questioning. If you find yourself in a conversation discussing, say, *Crime and Punishment* (my favorite book), and have no knowledge or interest in the subject but want to hold your own in a long and painful car ride with me, the better questions to ask might be:

- What do you think *Crime and Punishment* is *really* about?
- Why do you think it was written?
- *Crime and Punishment?* Oh, that's interesting. How does it align with your personal experience in the justice system, Mr. Gowdy?
- What about *Crime and Punishment* do you like?

A bad question is almost always better than a false declarative assertion. I was listening to a recording of an Easter sermon and the preacher placed Luke in the room for the Last Supper. *Luke? Really?* He wasn't around during that time and if he was, he definitely wasn't one of the Twelve Disciples. It would have been far better had the preacher posed it as a question. "Was Luke there?" "Can you help me name the Disciples?" "How would you feel being in the room where the Last Supper took place?" You have an out with questions—all you were seeking was more information. You lose your jury when you make affirmative, declarative statements if those statements are either wrong or unproven. You are welcome to preface those statements with "in my opinion," but the presence of Luke at the Last Supper is not really open for opinion, is it?

When you're a preacher, your job to persuade is, quite literally, to convert. That's a tough gig and it's a big burden of proof to carry. A declarative statement like that could cause the listener to discredit your whole persuasive attempt and immediately stop listening to whatever it is that follows, no matter how innocent the mistake or how compelling the remainder of your point.

Does it really matter if a preacher makes an honest mistake and places one of the authors of the four Gospels in a room where many may have assumed he was anyway? Probably not. Perhaps my reaction to placing Luke at the Last Supper was a projection of my own spiritual battle onto someone who is supposed to know more than I do. But while some mistakes in life are free, some cost you your life, and many are somewhere in the middle, there are those mistakes that force you to confront your own mental demons and lead you into deeper introspection. *What does this innocuous but obvious mistake mean to a listener on the edge? What other factual discrepancies may occur when spreading what is supposed to be biblical truth?* That's when the questions move inward.

SELF-DIRECTED AND SELF-PERSUADED

Remember my smart medical doctor father? Well, he loves South Carolina Gamecock football more than anything in life. I am pretty sure he loves South Carolina Gamecock football more than he loves my three sisters and me (although in his defense he does deny that). He would pile us into a wood-paneled station wagon six hours before kickoff so we could tailgate leisurely and be in the stands to watch . . . the band warm up. Yes, you read that correctly. Not to watch the players warm up. To watch the *band* warm up before the players even took the field. It was an all-day Saturday affair and we were never late. Except once.

We pulled out of the driveway of our home on the east side of Spartanburg and took a right rather than a left to head toward the interstate and Columbia for the game. We took another right and wound up on the road where Lana and Randy Mahaffey lived with their two sons, Clay and David. Clay and David were just a little bit younger than I was, and I knew them very well. Lana and Randy were my parents' closest friends. Both Lana and Randy were schoolteachers. The Mahaffeys went to the same church we attended. Randy was and remains a phenomenal golfer—even into his eighties. Countless nights he would watch me swing a club under a streetlight trying to help me master the game. The "professor," we call him. He taught high school physics and made it fun, which is really hard to do. Lana taught high school English and part of my love for reading came from the short stories I read in her class. Our backyards touched each another—backyards big enough for a full-field football game. Even though Clay and David were a little younger, we still played together, and when I hit my early teens I even babysat for them.

Why in the world was Dad stopping by their house on game day? Why was Mom sitting in the front seat with a blank stare on her face? Why wouldn't Mom answer when we asked how much longer Dad would be inside? Why were tears streaming down Mom's face?

Dad was inside telling his best friend and my mom's best friend that their younger son, David, had leukemia.

The who, what, when, where, and how questions that make up so much of life become so small and inconsequential in the face of the toughest question of all: *Why?*

David Mahaffey fought but ultimately died, and with him

died that childhood innocence each of us enjoys for at least a season of life. For me, that innocence would be replaced with a life's worth of questions.

We moved to another house in Spartanburg about a mile away. This new house had three stories, a clothes chute where we could drop clothes from the top floor and they would magically appear in the basement, and the most important feature of all for me—a small coat closet where no one would think to look for me. That's where the inner dialogue began:

Where did we come from? Was there a reservoir of souls God picked from? How did I get picked for this family? Are the souls recycled? Could David come back as someone else's son? Where was he now? Why didn't I have a brother? Why did God take David when Lana and Randy only had two children? Why not take me or one of my sisters? My parents would still have three children if He did that?

No, I did not necessarily like cutting the grass for hours, but I could talk to myself and that I did like. No, I did not like riding in the third seat of the station wagon by myself, but I could talk to myself, and that I did like. No, I did not like getting up at 4:00 A.M. to deliver newspapers on a motorized bicycle, but there was no one else up, and I could talk to myself, and that I did like.

That dialogue continues to this day. I am constantly asking myself questions and rehearsing the questions I would like to ask others. Every closing argument ever given in a courtroom was given pushing a lawnmower weeks before. Every speech ever given in Congress was first given driving alone to and from the airport in my truck. I play it out in my head before it ever happens in real life. How do I ask that? What if she says this? Where do you pivot to if that is the answer? How can you process a "yes" or "no" with equal speed and acuity?

So, yes, asking questions was the natural and probable convergence of several factors: (1) It was a lack of confidence in my own abilities, (2) it was first the realization and subsequently an acknowledgment of what human nature is at its core (everyone is begging to be heard, so I've got the leg up if I just decide to shut up and listen), (3) it was hours spent in an endless inner dialogue trying to understand what I believed, why I believed it, and whether those beliefs could withstand the cauldron of public display, and, lastly, (4) over the course of time, it became a devilish way to either turn the tables during a conversation or lower the tensions and avoid the impending conflict. Asking questions just seemed the best way to communicate and persuade while lowering the risk of exposing any personal weaknesses.

But most of all, questions have been the way I persuaded others for as long as I can remember because questions have been the way I persuaded myself for as long as I can remember.

3 X 0 = 3

I told you Lana and Randy Mahaffey had two sons: Clay and David. Clay continues to be a friend to this day. We don't play golf as much as we used to. He's long since married (to a wonderful woman named Stacey). He went to Clemson University (no one is perfect) and became an engineer. There is a certain symmetry that begins to emerge in life if you look closely for it. Clay's father helped instill a lifelong love of golf in me. I was present when Clay had his first hole in one. It's why I call him "Ace" instead of Clay, and no one else does.

Clay and Stacey have children of their own. They named their first son David. David Mahaffey the second. This David Mahaffey is a strong, smart college kid. He's also a golfer and worked at the golf course where our two families have played countless rounds together for well over half a century.

David Mahaffey scored higher on the math section of the

SAT than I did in all sections combined. Don't laugh. He probably scored higher than you did too. So, of course, I am going to engage him in a conversation about math, right? I like challenges. I like taking on Goliath.

Asking myself math questions is easy: I don't know whether my answers are right or not. How hard can that conversation be? But asking questions of someone good at math, that's a challenge. Persuading someone who is more knowledgeable than I am, now that is what the art of persuasion is all about.

"What is 3 x 0?" I asked the young David Mahaffey.

He looked at me like I had lost my mind. "It's zero, Mr. Gowdy. Everyone knows that."

"I don't know about that, David. I don't think it is. 0 x 3 is 0, I agree. But 3 x 0 is not."

"I'm sorry, Mr. Gowdy, but it is."

"Says who?"

"Says everyone, Mr. Gowdy."

"Am I not someone, David? Are you minimizing my existence because I have a different view of nothingness than you do? Am I not someone? Do I not matter, David?"

"Uh, Mr. Gowdy, anything times zero is zero," David replied.

"No, David, I don't believe that. 3 x 0 is 3. You cannot make what I had disappear. I had 3 of something. I multiplied it by nothing but my 3 did not disappear, and I am not going to allow you to act as if something doesn't exist when you conceded in the equation that it did. I can't allow that. I won't stand for that. It would be wrong, David. Would you want me to do that, David? Would you want me to act as if something that exists does not exist?"

By this time, the head golf professional, both assistant golf professionals, and a half dozen cart room workers were standing around us. I live for these moments!

"David, I love you. I've known your family forever. Your grandfather taught me physics. Your grandmother taught me English. I was there when your father had his first hole in one. By the way, are you telling me your father didn't really have a hole in one because you weren't present for it? Is that what you mean by nothing? 0 x 3 is zero, I concede. I started with nothing and nothing times 3 is still nothing. But 3 x 0 is not nothing. I have 3 of something. Are you saying I don't? Are you denying that I have 3 of something? Are you suspending reality because you want to win a math argument in front of your peers? David, where is my 3? Where did it go? How can you act as if it did not exist? There is no math formula you can devise that will convince me to ignore something I know existed. You cannot will it away and I am frankly surprised and disappointed you would try. Where is my 3, David?!"

Poor David Mahaffey. How do you argue with a madman? How do you argue math with a man who thinks the order in which one structures 3 x 0, versus 0 x 3, will really impact the answer? David looked at me as I finished cleaning my last golf club and said, "Mr. Gowdy, I don't have an answer for you but I know I am right. I am going to go home and ask my parents to help me frame an answer, but I know full well anything times zero is zero. I just can't explain it right now."

As I pulled out of the parking lot of the golf course, the symmetry of life overwhelmed me on so many levels.

First, let's don't overlook the obvious—the guy who made a "D" in his last high school math class and failed out of all his college math courses held his own with a math genius. Let's at least celebrate that for a moment!

But the real symmetry was the more than fifty years of connectivity between the Mahaffey family and the Gowdy family. If you can remember one thing, remember that the art of persuasion is not about winning people over. It's about bringing people closer together. The power of questions (if used correctly) is that there is an inherent give-and-take—equal parts speaking *and* listening. Sure, I could have asked David how baseball and golf were going. I could have asked him what he was going to major in. But I decided to question him relentlessly on what happened to my original 3. I wanted this young man who was good at math to be good at communication. You know the answer is zero. Convince me it is zero. Do it with an audience. Do it under pressure. Persuade. Communicate. Advocate. Connect.

I am sure David did go home that night and ask his parents how to communicate a simple concept to someone who should know it already. But isn't that life? Isn't that what we all want to do? Communicate effectively. Passionately.

I am certain the Mahaffeys had a great laugh at home that night wondering how someone could ever be elected to Congress with so little knowledge of basic mathematical truths. And I have no doubt that Clay said at some point, "This explains a lot about our nation's fiscal policy that our congressman doesn't know math."

There are so few things I fully understand. Why I am here on this earth. Why bad things happen to good people. The idea of "All things (no matter how dark or evil) work together for good." I have not fully persuaded myself of that and I suspect I never will. But I *have* persuaded myself that it's okay to let that question go and enjoy the art of asking questions and the art of persuasion as a way to connect and communicate. Those questions I asked myself in a pitch-black closet on the eastside of Spartanburg about the first David Mahaffey seem to make a little more sense now than they did back then. I learned not to shy away from difficult questions, because oftentimes they will lead you to truth.

You might ask some *really* stupid questions at first. Like

"What color is the blue bag?" or "Was my hometown of Spartanburg named for Sparta?" or "What is 3 x 0?" But keep asking questions. First of yourself. Then of others. Ask questions about your existence, about everyone, and everything. The person you end up persuading may wind up being yourself, and sometimes that is the toughest jury of all.

CHAPTER 2

THE SUBTLE ART OF PERSUASION

INCREMENTAL MOVEMENTS

It began with a quick trip around the back of Senator Tim Scott's car. We were at a restaurant in Charleston, South Carolina, heading to a quick lunch. US SENATOR 2 was on the license plate of his sedan.

"What are you doing with that on your license plate?" I jeered. "People are going to see you speeding, or changing lanes without a signal, or listening to your music too loud and call local television or radio and turn you in. That doesn't even account for those who didn't like the way you voted on some bill and will run their key down the side of your car. What were you thinking getting a vanity plate?"

He laughed, but only a little. "How many times were you stopped last year by the police, Trey?" he asked.

"Just once driving back from Aiken, I think."

"Were you scared?"

"I was scared my insurance would go up but that's it."

His mood had changed from the ubiquitously cheery Tim Scott to the more pensive, serious version of himself. "Trey, I was stopped seven times in one year as an elected official. Seven. I want the officers to know I am not a threat to them so nothing bad happens to me. I want to be safe, Trey, and stay alive."

Tim Scott is one of the most gentle-spirited, kind, and respectful people I have ever known in my time on this earth. He is kind to everyone. He is respectful to everyone. He has a permanent smile on his face. What is he talking about wanting officers to know he isn't a "threat to them so nothing bad happens" to him?

Thus began the journey of my own persuasion—at the hands of someone dear to me—on an issue as significant as criminal justice reform, racism, and the way certain communities view law enforcement. The persuasion started that afternoon with a mere question: *How many times had I been stopped by law enforcement in the last year?*

Because I care about him, I cared what his answer was to that same question and what his experiences had been. Because of the measured, factual way he presented his own life experience, it had the authenticity to move me. One time versus seven times. That day began a yearlong odyssey of being persuaded by the fact that even a U.S. senator had a different experience with law enforcement because he was black. The change was incremental. The change took time. But I was eventually changed.

This is persuasion.

Tim Scott persuaded me to look at law enforcement through the eyes of others, not just the eyes of a white doctor's son who worked as a prosecutor and had only positive experiences with men and women in blue. He persuaded me to consider why communities of color are less likely to cooperate, less likely to give the benefit of the doubt to the police, and less likely to ac-

cept blindly law enforcement's view in officer-involved shootings. He moved me from one position to another—subtly,
incrementally—but it was real and therefore long-lasting.

In the process of persuading me, he modeled the characteristic most necessary to be a compelling advocate or messenger,
which is the willingness to be persuaded or convinced himself.
You will not hear Tim Scott use the phrase "routine traffic
stop" when referring to law enforcement. Not anymore, you
won't. You will not hear Tim Scott refer to a "domestic violence 911 call" as a "normal call" in the course of a law enforcement officer's day. Tim Scott will tell you that he was persuaded
to believe there is no such thing as a "routine traffic stop" when
you are the one initiating the stop. He will tell you that despite
the frequency with which law enforcement responds to 911
calls, those are some of the most dangerous calls responded to
for all involved. His own vocabulary exemplifies his ability to
ask himself important questions and his *personal* persuadability.

Through the process of persuading me to look at how communities of color view our justice system and law enforcement,
he did the single more persuasive thing you can do. He allowed
himself to take a fresh look as well—at the life of a police officer, at the risks associated with those "routine" calls, and at
what goes through an officer's mind when he or she makes a
traffic stop not knowing what is going to happen when the
door slightly opens on the driver's side.

He moved me—he moved himself—from one perspective
to a new one. There was a distinct change and that is what the
art of persuasion is all about.

THE MOST PERSUASIVE ARE THE PERSUADABLE

I want you to ask yourself a question in the privacy of your own
conscience—and answer it truthfully: Are you genuinely open

to moving on a position, of altering the way you look at an issue, or considering a different vantage point?

If you are not open to doing that, what makes you think others will be? I'm not asking you to surrender a deeply held conviction. Just be open to looking at that conviction in a different way.

I'll give you an example.

I sought the death penalty more than half a dozen times as a prosecutor. In the old days of youth, if you asked me why I supported the death penalty, I would tell you it's a deterrent for others who are contemplating taking a life. I might have even argued it was biblically sound. It seemed to make sense as a youth: Take a life, forfeit a life, end someone's dreams, surrender your own—there seemed a certain symmetry to that and as a young person symmetry was enough.

And then in my late teens and early twenties I persuaded myself that I was wrong—that the death penalty was actually *not* just and was not biblically defensible. More than convincing myself, I sought to convince others. While I was attending college in Texas, my mother would send me the local Spartanburg paper so I could keep up with what was going on back home. One paper she sent included a story that the local solicitor was seeking the death penalty for a man named Jesse Keith Brown. I knew nothing about the facts, nothing about the criminal history of the person accused of committing the crime, and nothing about the circumstances of the victim's life or those left to mourn his loss. Those are all highly relevant facts but not to a twenty-year-old who was seeking a different kind of symmetry from his youth. So, I wrote the solicitor and asked him to please reconsider his decision to seek the death penalty in this case.

The letter was written in print, not cursive, on a piece of notebook paper, and it was polite but more conclusory than analytical. How do I recall that so well, you ask? Because I wound up running for solicitor against the very man to whom that letter was sent and that letter wound on up the front page of our local paper a week before the election! The thirty-five-year-old version of myself was reading the beliefs of the twenty-year-old version of myself and was aghast at my poor handwriting, among other things. I was certain this bid for elected office was doomed. There it was, in black and white, that the person running for solicitor, the chief prosecutor who would in turn make decisions as to whether or not to seek the death penalty, did not believe in the death penalty as a college student.

Life has a way of making you evaluate and reevaluate what you believe and why you believe it. The twenty-year-old Trey, musing about the meaning of life and death, turned into a thirty-five-year-old Trey who had a wife, two children, and an empty spot in his soul left by the murder of a family friend. The thirty-five-year-old version of myself had experienced the impossible task of explaining to a mother how and why her son was killed for cooperating as a witness in a drug case I was prosecuting at the U.S. Attorney's Office. Life happens, we change, and people are accepting of that change so long as we provide them with plausible and thoughtful explanations.

And now I have two children in their twenties, one of whom is in law school and going through some of the same internal dialogue I experienced when I was her age. She knows her father prosecuted death penalty cases and she knows that at one point in life I did not believe in the death penalty, so she wants to know where I am on the issue today. It's my belief as fifty-five-year-old Trey that some crimes are just so heinous and committed by persons with such extensive criminal histories of ignoring the pain caused to others that it is the only appropriate punishment. Should it be few and far between? Yes. Should it be reserved for particularly heinous cases involving unmitigated depravity with little to no mitigation on the defendant's side? Yes.

This is where I've landed in my own internal persuasion, and I'm always willing to listen to alternative arguments—even if those arguments are coming exclusively from within my own mind.

So, are you persuadable yourself? Are you willing to listen to other arguments rooted in fact and logic? Are you open to a new way of thinking or listening? If you are, you have taken the longest step in the path toward the art of persuasion. If you are not, within the candor of your own mind, ask yourself: What *could* persuade you?

When you yourself are persuadable, that means you are open to new facts, new ideas, new perspectives. Being persuadable is not about being gullible, naïve, or weak; it means you have a high desire and capacity for more information and you don't limit yourself. When you are persuadable, you have asked yourself difficult questions and have looked at every side of the argument in an effort to seek truth, and anytime you seek truth, you often change your perspective. On the other hand, when you seek merely to be right or win, more often than not, you're far from the truth. Persuadable people choose the former— they seek truth and look at all sides of issues, which makes them not only empathetic but master persuaders.

WHAT PERSUASION IS VS. WHAT IT'S NOT

The courtroom is both the easiest and most difficult forum in which to persuade. It is easy because the jury, the group you are trying to persuade, *has* to be open-minded, or else they cannot serve on the jury. It is really the one indispensable characteristic necessary to serve. The more dogmatic you are, the less likely you are to be chosen by either side picking the jury.

It is difficult in the courtroom because you must convince all twelve jurors and you must do so by a very high level of convincing. In other words, you have to persuade *beyond a reasonable doubt*. Beyond a reasonable doubt is a difficult concept to grasp, so we sometimes substitute the phrase "firmly convinced." You must firmly convince all twelve jurors of the same thing to get a guilty verdict in a criminal case.

Think about it.

Winning over 65 percent of the people you are talking to in politics is considered a *landslide*. They will write ballads about you. They may etch you into Mount Rushmore. You might even get your face on the crisp dollar bill. Winning 65 percent of your conversations in life is pretty doggone good too. Imagine getting to pick the restaurant or movie 65 percent of the time. In a courtroom, you lose every time if all you can do is convince 65 percent of the people. Even convincing 99 percent of the people is failure in a courtroom. It's 100 percent or you lose.

So, what do you think of when you think of persuasion? Which words enter your mind? Do you think in terms of forcing someone to adopt your position? Do you think in terms of winning the argument? Do you think of having vastly superior debate and rhetorical skills? I used to confuse persuasion with arguing or pushing someone to do something, but nearly thirty years of practicing the art of persuasion has given me a decidedly different perspective.

Persuasion is not coercion.

Persuasion is not wearing someone down until they finally come around to your way of thinking. There is an old cliché: "You can lead a horse to water but you cannot make him drink." Persuading someone on any topic of significance is much like that. You drive the person with your declarative statements, your questions, your demeanor, your authenticity, and your experience to reach the conclusion on his or her own. You open pathways toward the destination you preordained, even cutting off escape routes, where if the person simply keeps walking, keeps searching, keeps talking, he or she will ultimately wind up where you want them to—even if they think it was their decision all along.

True and artful persuasion is teaching without either of you identifying who is the teacher and who is the student.

Persuasion is not debating.

Despite popular opinion, the best debaters do not make the best politicians, they do not make the best attorneys, and they certainly are not the best at persuading. Debating is science. Persuasion is art. In a debate you watch the clock to know when it is your turn to talk. In persuasion there is no clock; there is an acquired sense of when there is an opening and an even more acquired sense of when to step into that opening. Debating is for the best talker. Persuasion is for the better listener. Ted Cruz would be considered a very skilled political debater. Elizabeth Warren would be as well. They have an almost scientific way of structuring their arguments. They seem to have command of the facts and are confident in their rhetorical skills.

Some of the members of Congress I found most persuasive would not win debating contests, but they would also not *enter* debating contests. Kevin McCarthy was persuasive because I knew he would be honest about the legislation we were discussing, even if it meant I was not able to vote the way he wanted me to. John Ratcliffe was persuasive because he was willing to entertain the notion that perhaps there was a better way to accomplish a shared goal. Elise Stefanik was persuasive because she was humble, thoughtful, and genuine. Peter Welch was persuasive because he was such a good, active, and engaged listener. Jim Himes was persuasive because he yielded ground when the ground should be yielded and actively looked for areas of agreement.

The same is true in life. Those who can move us the most often make grammatical mistakes, they may tell jokes that fall flat, or they may lose their place in their PowerPoint presentation and have to pause for a moment, but they are real. They are genuine.

In the courtroom, I did not fear the smartest defense attorneys. I did not fear the loudest defense attorneys. I did not fear the defense attorneys who seemed to know the rules of evidence the best. I feared those defense attorneys who connected with the jury on a personal level and who left the jury believing this defense attorney will never intentionally mislead them, and those defense attorneys who had an innate sense of knowing exactly what the jury's questions were even though the jury could not verbalize those questions. Between skill and authenticity, pick authenticity. Between technical superiority and likability, pick likability. Between debate and persuasion, pick persuasion.

Persuasion is not arguing.
I know lots of people who are good at arguing. They can turn the most enjoyable of meals into a combat zone because they simply love to argue. Arguing is one declarative statement after another, frequently in pitched tones, oftentimes talking over the person with whom they are purporting to communicate. Arguing is not persuasive—arguing is arguing. Arguments cannot be won, and they are not designed to be won. Arguments are designed to inflame, and while they are unavoidable in life,

that does not mean they should not be minimized. What you really want, and what has the potential to be far more long-lasting, is that beautiful kind of communication that moves all of those involved.

I know they call them "closing arguments" in the court-room. But trust me—having done more than I can count, there is nothing argumentative about the last statements made in a courtroom. It is pure movement via storytelling. You are attempting to move people who did not know you or one another days earlier toward finding consensus even in the midst of negativity and pain. They do not want to be yelled at. They want to be cajoled. They do not want to be lectured to. They want to be reasoned with. They do not want to be told what to do (people inherently resist that). They want to be led by someone they trust in a direction they are thinking about going anyway or a reason to change course that is rooted in fact and logic.

Because there is a keen difference between power and influence. You may have the *power* to force your son or daughter to stay home on a Friday evening. But *influence* can work even better with longer-lasting outcomes (and result in children that—wait for it—actually *like* you).

If we live long enough, arguments will find us. They're unavoidable. Sometimes we just have bad days or the person with whom we are communicating is making life impossible for us. But to the extent that we can substitute persuasion for argument in our everyday lives, those lives will be enhanced and better lived. Whether it's convincing someone to gain some perspective about varying communities, selling a project to a skeptical co-worker, getting the person on the plane to switch seats with you so you can sit by your spouse, or getting your parents to acknowledge the fact that, yes, Bono really is a poet, real life is ripe for everyday persuasion.

Persuasion is incremental.

Think of persuasion as change. Think of persuasion as movement. Think of persuasion as incremental. The scale, what can be effectively measured, will come later (Chapter 5, to be exact), but for now, just embrace that persuasion is some migration toward a different place.

Wholesale conversions do occur—and perhaps they receive a disproportionate amount of attention—but they are rare. There are examples of people moving from one deeply held set of religious convictions to another vastly different set. There are examples of progressives becoming conservatives and conservatives becoming progressives. There are examples of Dallas Cowboy fans becoming Washington Redskin fans, but I can think of only one in my lifetime, and, unfortunately for me, it was my father who made that precipitous fall from America's Team to Washington.

You will have more success in slight changes, slight movements, subtle pushes and pulls.

Persuasion is getting a spouse to watch a sporting event rather than a romantic comedy. Persuasion is making sure that if the household adds the SEC Network, we are also going to add the Hallmark Channel. Persuasion is about getting your boss to give you a commission that rewards your hard work rather than a mere bump in salary to reflect your longevity. Persuasion is getting your teenager to come in at 10:00 P.M. instead of 11:00 P.M. because they have a busy schedule the next day. Those are the decisions and movements life is made of: those small, incremental movements from neutrality to a new position, from a previously held position to another position, or simply looking at a familiar issue in a slightly different way.

In politics, the movement is typically *very* small. That is just the reality of where we are in the current political environment.

Absolute persuasion is quite difficult to achieve. There are exceptions that are worth noting, but the capacity to persuade is slight because, in part, the willingness to be persuaded is slight.

Kyrsten Sinema is a progressive U.S. senator from Arizona. She's a Democrat through and through. She is also remarkable because she is persuadable. When we both served in the House, Senator Sinema would come find me on the floor of the House, sit down beside me, and say, "I am thinking of voting for this bill. Let's talk about it." She was genuinely undecided and willing to consider opposing arguments. In turn, she had an expectation that you would listen without prejudice when she offered you her perspective on an issue. There were a handful of other House members open to trying to persuade or be persuaded. But it was rare (and refreshing).

If the potential for significant change as it relates to politics is slight in the hallways of Congress, it is likely to be equally slight in the hallways of your own home if the topic is overtly political in nature. For example, the power of and need for education is something we can all agree on, parent and child alike. What constitutes equality in access to education coupled with who sets the curriculum coupled with whether college should be "free" (and defining what "free" means)—well, those are all topics on which the consensus can dissipate quickly. That conversation about education, rooted in fact and civility, can and should be had, but it is admittedly more difficult to persuade when the issue moves from the power of education to the empowering of paying for that education, because those issues can be seen as veering toward the political.

In real life, we persuade people all of the time whether we are aware of what we are doing or not. *Should we eat out or in tonight? Should we move across town or across the country? Should we get a dog or a cat? Can you cut the grass (finally)? Will you listen to this song?* It is much more difficult to, say, change their opinion on criminal justice reform.

When attempting to persuade someone about a topic on which they already have a firm stance, it is important to know the facts about the topic and get to know your audience and what is important to them. Tim Scott presented facts and evidence that caused me to question my position and, because he knew me and knew my position on criminal justice reform, he was able to subtly ask questions that continued to challenge me on that topic. He moved me authentically, which is the best, and arguably only, way to persuade.

The world will be a quieter, less hostile place if we replace the desire to shout with the desire to be heard, if we replace the desire to win the argument with the desire to move the person who wants to argue, and if we reserve for ourselves some of the toughest questions we can conjure up.

CHAPTER 3

KNOW THE OBJECTIVE, KNOW THE FACTS, KNOW THYSELF!

THE 30-MINUTE JURY

Dana Satterfield was a beautiful young mother and wife. She had a hair salon in Roebuck, South Carolina. She worked hard and was beloved by her family and her customers.

The first image of Dana I saw was her lifeless, partially nude body hanging by the strap of a cosmetics bag from the top of a water heater in the bathroom of her salon that she operated out of her mobile home.

She was killed in July 1995. The case went unsolved for a decade. I still clearly remember the day Sheriff Chuck Wright called me to tell me that, more than ten years after her murder, they were ready to make an arrest. "Trey, are you sitting down?" he asked. I wasn't. I was out of town playing in a golf tournament with some friends, but my friend Sheriff Wright didn't even give me a chance to sit down before he screamed into the phone, "We are ready to make an arrest in Dana Satterfield's murder!"

In 1995, when Dana was killed, Chuck Wright was not the

sheriff and I was not the solicitor but you could not be alive in upstate South Carolina without knowing about her case. It dominated the media in the aftermath of the discovery of her body. Wild theories abounded about who killed her, including theories about her own husband and rumors about a local elected official. Murder is not rare, sadly. But the murder of a young woman in her shop in a sleepy part of our county right off a major highway? That was rare. And the longer the case went unsolved, the more rumors flooded our hometown and the longer the nightmare for her family went on.

Jonathan Vick was arrested for Dana's murder. He would have been seventeen years old at the time—a rising senior in high school. He had no criminal record but his DNA was found in her shop. Why? Why was he there? Did they know each other? What will the defense attorney do with the fact that Dana and her husband were, at the time, having marital discord? Where was the out-of-town door-to-door saleswoman who claimed to see someone running from the shop at about the time of the murder? Could we find her ten years later? Was she even alive? What do we do with the hundreds of leads and the countless other suspects who were investigated with varying degrees of success? More than anything, how do we overcome the note in the lead detective's file that read "Jonathan Vick did not commit this murder"?

We have all seen people we care about become preoccupied, bordering on obsessed with things. Obsessed with getting into a certain school. Obsessed with winning the affection of a certain young man or woman. Obsessed with a certain job, or car, or relationship. There is a fine line between diligence and obsession. If there is ever anything for which obsession would be understandable, it would be finding justice for a young mother killed in her place of business by a seventeen-year-old stranger.

The trial was set for the fall of 2006, so there was about a year between the arrest and the trial. I spent that year learning every single solitary fact I could about Dana and her case. And I spent even more time anticipating what the defense would do to defend Jonathan Vick.

Back then, in the mid-2000s, my parents would take the whole family to the beach for a week in the summer. My kids were thirteen and nine, respectively, at the time. No doubt they loved playing on the beach, riding waves, and building sand-castles with their mother. But it was as if their mother, my wife, was a single parent that week. Sure, I was physically there. But I wasn't *really* there. I was neck deep in boxes of material I took to the beach so I could do a good job for Dana Satterfield and her family later that fall. I worked hard on all of my cases, espe-cially my murder cases. But I never worked as hard on any case as I did on Dana Satterfield's murder. Part of that was because I knew the defense would blame her husband and there is noth-ing worse in the world than losing your wife and then being wrongly blamed for her murder. Part of it was for Dana's chil-dren and especially her daughter Ashley, who had become a young woman by then, and the unsolved murder of her mother had dominated her life for as long as she could remember. But mostly I worked hard for Dana, because I would want someone to work hard if someone I cared about was victimized the way she was murdered, assaulted, partially disrobed, and staged to be hanging from a water heater.

I became obsessed. I spent hours uncovering every bit of information I could gather. Every car ride, every walk on the golf course, every spare moment was dominated by thinking through the facts, reflecting on how I was going to prepare to present those facts, and anticipating every possible outcome— every single word that would come out of the mouth of the defense attorney or Jonathan Vick himself and preconceiving the appropriate response or rebuttal.

Hours of asking myself:

Vick's DNA was on her stomach but nowhere else—how did it get there?

Will Vick claim it was planted or that there was an error in processing the crime scene? Would he say that he was a customer and the DNA was left from an earlier visit? Would he say he engaged in consensual sex and the "real killer" must have come in afterward?

How do we handle the marital difficulties? I was convinced Dana's husband had nothing to do with her murder. Convinced. I was also convinced that given his size, it was physically impossible for him to climb out of a small window in a mobile home and exit the way the killer did. But how do I convince a jury of that and do it in a respectful but thorough and honest way? There would be tough questions for Dana's husband. How do we ask the tough questions but do it without making him unsympathetic? How do we do it first, during our case, so the jury does not believe we are hiding something? It's usually better to draw out potentially negative information on your own as the prosecutor, and not wait for the defense attorney to do it, because it builds trust with the jury. It's called "taking the sting out," but how do we do it in this case?

Where are the fingerprints? Vick's fingerprints were nowhere to be found in the beauty salon. Prosecutors and cops know everyone doesn't leave prints when they touch something and some prints can last a long time, but the average juror watches things like *CSI* and *Law and Order* where forensic evidence carries the day. That will be their expectation—forensic evidence—so how do we meet those expectations or explain the difference between TV and real life?

What about the hair? Hairs that were not a match for Vick were found on Dana. What does that mean? Did she take her clothes to a laundromat? Could the hair have come from that?

Does it corroborate the defense position that there were marital woes and therefore expose the prosecution to other potential murderers with motive? Hair found on the victim would need to be dealt with, but how? It was a singularly difficult thing to explain away—the presence of hair on Dana when the hair was not Jonathan Vick's.

I distinctly remember sitting on the front porch of that beach house looking at the same crime scene photos again and again. *Something is here, I just have to find it.* Meanwhile the two prosecutors who were handling the case with me—Barry J. Barnette and Cindy S. Crick—were doing the same thing. Barry thought like a scientist, which I needed, because I thought like an artist. Cindy was excellent at both. We would need Cindy and her skill in the courtroom if the defense was that Vick and Dana had consensual sex before the "real killer" came in. From both the crime scene photos and the forensic autopsy, we learned that Dana was menstruating at the time of her murder. Can we convince a jury that that would not be the time a young married mother would be having sex with a seventeen-year-old customer: in her shop, on a bathroom floor, while menstruating?

And then I saw it: pictures from the bathroom floor taken by law enforcement the night of the murder. The bathroom was on the other end of the salon from the work space where she cut clients' hair. Her body was at the top of the picture but my eyes were drawn to the bottom of the picture. Right near the door. Hair. Single strands of hair. But not hair clippings you would expect to find in a hair salon. These were pubic hairs you would expect to find in a public restroom on the floor. I had it. I had an explanation for why pubic hairs not belonging to Vick would be on her nude body. The hairs were hard to see. That picture would need to be magnified at trial. But they were there and that provided the answer to the most intractable trial issue we would face. She was dragged across the bathroom floor to the water heater and those pubic hairs found during the autopsy were on her from that. Those were not the hairs from the killer. Those were the hairs that stuck to her body as the killer dragged her across the floor.

I knew Jonathan Vick killed Dana Satterfield. But I also knew that typically seventeen-year-olds do not commit murder as their first crime. So why did he? What were we missing that would explain that his first foray into criminality was the violent murder of a young mother?

And then there was that note in the case file: *Jonathan Vick did not commit this crime.* That was pretty definitive. And it wasn't from the defendant's mother. It was from the lead detective investigating the case. How do we get around just how very wrong this detective wound up being?

What about the countless other leads pursued over the course of the past ten years? Law enforcement talked to scores of witnesses. They even talked to Vick shortly after the murder but did not pursue him as a suspect. How do we explain the thoroughness of the investigation without inviting reasonable doubt that maybe one of the other "suspects" really did commit the murder? After all, the lead detective wrote that Vick did not!

The jury was out less than thirty minutes. Not even long enough for a meal or a smoke break.

A jury verdict in less than thirty minutes might mean that the year I spent immersed in the Dana Satterfield murder case file wasn't necessary. Thirty minutes might mean I worried for over a year for no reason. Or maybe it was the exact opposite of that. Maybe because I spent a year of my life studying, preparing, anticipating, and worrying over every point and counterpoint during every car ride, every shower, every walk, that is why the jury needed less than thirty minutes to decide that, after ten years, Jonathan Vick did indeed murder Dana Satterfield.

Jonathan Vick was found guilty and sentenced to life imprisonment.

Dana Satterfield's murder case was not won in closing argument before the jury. It was won months and months before that. Months spent by three prosecutors putting our lives on hold for close to a year to know more about what happened the last night of her life than anyone else and then preparing for the most effective way to present that to twelve people who knew nothing about the case.

Do you know what it is you are trying to persuade someone of? I mean, do you *really* know it? Do you know the issue? Have you studied it thoroughly, examined every aspect of it, and cross-examined it in your own mind? If you truly want to move people to a new way of thinking, you not only must know exactly what you hope to accomplish with your persuasive efforts, but you must know the issue, fact pattern, or belief you are seeking movement on.

The people who live with me and work with me all know my favorite saying. They cringe when they sense I am about to quote it for the one trillionth time: "Chance favors the prepared mind." Louis Pasteur said it and it's true. Rarely does something just happen. Rarely do you just "luck" into something. Life rewards preparation. It is not a guarantee that you will succeed but it is the single best way to hedge your bets against failure. And where does that chance begin? It begins by gathering your facts.

GET THE FACTS STRAIGHT

A fact is something that actually exists and has an objective reality. Sometimes facts can be proven; sometimes they cannot be (which is frustrating but nonetheless true). A fact that cannot be proven impacts your ability to persuade but it does not diminish the existence of that fact. So, what are the facts? Can you separate fact from belief? Fact from opinion? Fact from theory? Fact from feeling? All of the above are essential components of life, but facts are the single most important foundational element for constructing a winning argument or position.

If your goal is to persuade, you must have full command of the facts. Have you done your homework? Have you separated out what you *feel* about tax rates from the *facts* about tax rates? Have you separated what you believe about majoring in sociology from the facts of what sociology majors can and cannot do with that degree? Sociology is a perfectly fine major or concentration of study. But if someone in your life says, "Sociology majors do better than other majors in law school," whether or not that is supported by facts is knowable. If someone says, "I believe sociology prepares you best for law school," that is a perfectly fine belief, but that belief would be subordinate to whatever the facts *are*. If someone says, "I feel sociology majors do well in law school," that is a perfectly fine expression of his or her emotion, but no matter how strongly he or she "feels" that, it is still subordinate to facts, and I would argue even subordinate to a belief. So, do you traffic in facts? Do you investigate your position or belief before you state it? How do you do so? How do you research your position before you adopt it?

When I was younger, most of what I believed, quite frankly, was because my parents or some other adult told me to believe it. My parents are smart, conscientious people, so I started with a presumption that their position was at least well-intentioned, even if it was based on belief, emotion, or thinking, as opposed to fact. My father is a medical doctor and that is a fact-centric vocation, so there was a heavy emphasis on facts undergirding whatever position he held. Additionally, both of my parents are also conservative and spiritual, which is a combination of fact, belief, thinking, and emotion. All of those things are worthy of being evaluated, reconsidered, and rearranged. But as I became an adult, I found that facts were, to me, easiest to either corroborate or contradict, so I preferred to focus on them.

In 1650 Oliver Cromwell, imploring the General Assembly of the Church of Scotland to step away from their pledge of allegiance to the royalist cause, said: "I beseech you in the bowels of Christ, think it possible that you may be mistaken."* In other words, *Consider the remote possibility you may be wrong.* I don't know how I feel about beseeching in the bowels of anything, but it's advice worth heeding regardless. How often do we reevaluate our positions? How often do we factor new information into our decision-making process? Sometimes a single fact can change your entire perspective on an issue.

If you knew as a fact that someone struck another person, you may conclude something. If you added the fact that it was in self-defense, you may conclude something different. If you added the fact that the person doing the striking was striking in defense of a child or other vulnerable person, you would likely conclude something very different. Facts impact conclusions. Facts are always subject to being discovered unless and until all facts are known and processed—so you've got to keep uncovering them.

I have a process I go through with myself any time I am on the verge of making some assertion of fact or trying to state a declarative point, and it's worth considering whether this process or paradigm would work for you too. If it doesn't, create

---

* Thomas Carlyle, ed., *Oliver Cromwell's Letters and Speeches,* vol. 1 (New York: Harper, 1855), 448.

your own. But have a process for reaching your conclusion and knowing what you are hoping to accomplish with that conclusion.

> First I ask myself, *What do I know?*
> Then, *How do I know it?*
> Last, *What are the limits of my knowledge?*

This is true with beliefs as well.

> *What do I believe?*
> *Why do I believe it?*
> *What other options have I considered?*

Let's take a certain issue where reasonable minds can and do differ: tax credits for parents who want to send their children to a nonpublic school. What do you know about this issue? What is the source of your information? What evidence exists that choosing schools is better for the students? What impact does the tax credit have on public schools? Do you view public schools as infrastructure that the broader community benefits from regardless of whether they participate in those schools? If you have a conclusion on this version of school choice, do you have a conclusion on whether that tax credit should be in addition to or in lieu of? In other words, if you send your student to a private school, should your tax dollars still go toward public education or should you receive a dollar-for-dollar credit to send your student where you want? If it's better for your student, is it better for other students? Is it better for the broader community? Is that your responsibility?

I don't know what my own perspective is on this issue. I see both sides of this issue. My best friend in politics, Tim Scott, has studied the issue exhaustively and feels passionately about matters of educational choice. My best friend in life, Terri, is a first-grade public school teacher. I am probably biased in some measure because of Terri's influence on me, but I can still make an effort to objectively gather facts and then draw reasonable conclusions from them.

Our generation has few excuses not to gather facts. I mean, come on! The information is available on our dadgum phones! Gone are the days of our parents periodically updating our encyclopedia collections. Gone are the days of waiting for the monthly trip to the public library. Information is available. Instantly.

Learned treatises. Studies. Academic works. Textbooks. Well-respected sources. We have immediate access to firsthand accounts of subject matter experts. Facts have never been easier for us to find. Perhaps it is a challenge to discern what is truly factual from what is not, but investing time to separate what is factually true from what is not is not a steep price to pay if your goal is to accurately and effectively communicate. Access to information and a skeptical mind are all you need, and both should be readily available.

Oftentimes in life, two people can look at precisely the same set of facts and draw diametrically different conclusions. That's precisely why we need to cultivate the art of persuasion. If we all looked at the same reservoir of facts and drew the same conclusions, we would likely not be a fifty-fifty family, community, or country. There is a difference between gathering information and effectively communicating that information. We all know people who are experts on specific subjects, but they could not persuade us to come indoors during a thunderstorm. Facts do not equal persuasion, but you will likely never be a consistently effective persuader if you have not first gathered the evidence needed. It is frustratingly true that oftentimes "evidence" exists on both sides of an issue. As I love to tell our daughter, Abigail, "There is evidence the earth is flat because the part I am standing on certainly is." But for abounding and obvious reasons, I would not like to take that piece of evidence and extrapolate it into a convincing argument.

FOR ALL INTENTS AND PURPOSES

So, you have your facts, you have drawn your conclusions, and you are ready to have a conversation with someone who either is not familiar with the issue at all or is as equally familiar with the issue as you are but has a different perspective. Now what?

You've got to ask yourself: *What is your purpose?*

Before you open your mouth—before you begin asking anyone anything—you have to put yourself through an extensive and deeply thoughtful round of self-inquiry. You've got to answer the following:

1. Do you want to start a fire, nurture a fire, or put out a fire?
2. Do you want to convert the person to your way of thinking?
3. Will you settle for the person with whom you are talking merely walking away with a different or new perspective and an agreement to take a fresh look at the issue?
4. Do you want to reach consensus on some points and agree to disagree on others? If so, what points are you willing to concede?
5. Do you just want to argue?

If you do not know your purpose, you are almost guaranteed not to achieve it. If you do not know going into a conversation what you are trying to accomplish, you will likely not accomplish anything productive. So, what is it you are hoping to do? Educate? Convert? Persuade subtly? Infuriate?

So, you know the facts.

You even know your purpose.

Now, know *thyself*!

How are you going to structure your argument? Are you leading with your best fact or are you waiting to build to an ending crescendo and leap into the arms of what the experts call recency, a belief that people are most likely to be persuaded by whoever they last hear from. There is a debate among people far smarter than I am about whether to structure arguments with your best lead or your best ending. One thing almost everyone will tell you is not to bury your best facts or arguments in the middle. I would tell you to start with your very best fact first. Then move to your third-best fact or argument and save your second-best fact for when you need it most. That is the approach I try to take. It's a little bit like playing cards. You don't play the King of Diamonds if the Ace of Diamonds hasn't been played unless it is in your own hand. In persuasion, because you get to stack your own deck and pick your own cards, you have the King and the Ace. Start with the Ace, move to the Queen, and hold the King for when you need a really good fact to pivot or respond with.

You have your facts. You have a sense of which ones are most significant, most compelling, and most likely to persuade. They're prioritized wisely. You have anticipated the weaknesses or gaps in your own knowledge—every point and counterpoint has already been thought through—and you have a plan for defending them or making your case without them. You have considered your purpose, your objective, and the path most likely to take you there.

Now and finally, how will you know when you arrive? Have you defined success in your own mind? Do you have an objective that is knowable and visible? Sometimes that objective is crystal clear, like in the courtroom with a particular verdict or in an election with the vote tally at the end of the night. In real life, it is more difficult to define success because, as we discussed, persuasion is movement and movement can be small. If your goal when you sit down to talk to your teenage daughter is to have her agree that piercings are a waste of her time and your money, that may be more difficult to achieve than simply getting her to wait until after the family holiday pictures are taken. If your goal is to get your son to make his bed like a marine, you have set a high goal. My goal was always just to get my son to pull the covers up a little so his mother at least thought he cared enough to try.

If you can keep a secret, I was never good at bathing our children when they were small. And because I was neither good at it nor particularly liked it, I had a different goal than you might imagine when Terri asked me to help back in the old days. My goal was to communicate a willingness to help by agreeing to do it, but then to do such a terrible job that she concluded it was easier to do it herself. Wow! I feel a weight has been lifted after confessing that after all these years! My goal was to "try," but for water to be everywhere and the kids' bedtime clothes soaking wet because I didn't move them far enough away and for the shampoo occasionally to be left in their hair and for them to be wide awake like they had a double espresso and unfit for nighttime reading and bedtime. So I had two objectives: communicate cooperation and ensure I was almost never asked to "cooperate" again. Success? Success was having Terri say with total exasperation, "You know, it might just be easier if I did it myself." "Well, if you say so, honey, but I am happy to help."

Hopefully your objective is not as nefarious and double-minded as mine was, but you need an objective and means of measuring success when you move toward persuasion.

While I was not good with children early in their years, as they got older, I got more helpful. Young people frequently come visit or call to discuss their goals as they transition from youth to young adulthood. What should I major in? Where should I go to law school? Should I intern for a committee of Congress or a member of Congress? All good questions, but I reverse the order: Where do you want to wind up? Do you want to be a judge or a state legislator? Do you want to teach or practice law? Do you want more money or more free time? Tell me where you want to wind up or what your objective is and then we can plot a course to help you achieve it. The same is true when it comes to persuasion. Know your objective, know your facts, know what success looks like, and it becomes much easier to plot the course to achieve it.

CHAPTER 4

KNOW YOUR JURY

THINK HOW THEY THINK

I cannot fully express to you how terrible I was in front of a jury when I began my legal career. I cringe thinking back on those early days. I was nervous. I was unsure. I was trying to follow a script rather than engage in the art of communicating with my fellow citizens.

Making matters worse, my first trial was in front of a federal judge with a reputation for cruel and unusual toughness bordering on torture. The Honorable George Ross Anderson, Jr., United States District Court Judge. The name struck fear in the hearts of lawyers across South Carolina. He had been a phenomenal trial attorney in his own right in Anderson, South Carolina, before being appointed to the federal bench. So he had exceedingly high expectations of everyone, especially his former law clerks. And I had been his law clerk longer than anyone else had been his law clerk, so his expectations were *very* high. Law clerks are like children to judges. And Judge Anderson was no different. Imagine Judge Anderson as a parent watching his "children" in a school spelling bee, not with a smile and nervous joy but with a bullwhip in one hand and a machete in the other. He expected a lot from his law clerks.

I was so nervous trying cases in front of him that I convinced my wife that we should name the daughter we were expecting after him to dampen the fallout from whatever dumb things I was likely to do in his courtroom now that I was trying cases as a lawyer. That's a true story. Our daughter is named Abigail Anderson Gowdy and the Anderson was after the Honorable George Ross Anderson, Jr., himself. Honestly, I would have named our daughter "George" or "Ross" if my wife had let me just to give myself some wiggle room if I found myself in his courtroom significantly underperforming.

"Honey, I think we should name our daughter George," I remember suggesting.

"Well, we are not" was her response.

"Can we at least talk about it?"

"We just did, and we are not ever going to talk about it again! We are not naming a girl George or Ross."

"Well, how about Judge?"

"No! Can you imagine making a girl grow up with the name George or Judge?!"

"Can you imagine me having to try cases in front of Judge Anderson without a safety net? She can change her name later if she wants to, but for a couple of years at least it would help me to tell Judge Anderson that 'our daughter, George Ross Anderson Gowdy, Jr., says hello'! I mean, she's not even born yet. No one is going to make fun of her until she gets to preschool. We can change it later if George isn't working for her."

By this time my wife had not only left the room, but left the small house we were living in. Apparently, that conversation was over. So much for newly married couples discussing everything with an open mind! My wife did agree to "Anderson" as a middle name because even she—in the quietness of her own heart—knew my life was in danger trying cases in front of the Honorable George Ross Anderson, Jr.

So I tried my first case in front of him. And it was worse than I had prepared for. I would glance over at the bench and see his eyes closed with his head resting in his hand. I prayed he was asleep, but most people do not use their other hand to pull their hair out of the top of their head if they are asleep, and they do not make guttural sounds like a wounded jackal either.

The trial ended and the jury found the defendant guilty. I don't know how or why. It was in spite of my performance as the prosecutor and not because of it.

Judge Anderson sent word that he wanted to see me back in his chambers before I left. This would be the end. I began writing a note to my wife telling her one more time that I loved her and to tell our children not to go to law school.

The door to his chamber flew open and I heard the word "NOW!" screamed louder than an EF5 tornado.

I walked back behind the courtroom, past my old desk where I sat when I clerked for him, and stood with my head down in his office. I knew this was going to be the end of my life.

"Son," he began, "I grew up on Equinox Mill. My parents were poor. Everyone I knew was poor. I went to college at night because I had to work during the day. I worked three jobs to put myself through law school. You, on the other hand, were a doctor's son. Life is not the country club playing golf. Life, real life, is in this courtroom. Regular people with regular hopes, dreams, and fears. You have to learn how to talk to regular people. Normal people. Everyday people. I love you, son. You have a chance to be good, but not unless you learn something about people. Head on home, now. I know you don't drink, but it might do you good to stop in a bar sometime. Sit down and listen to real people. How they think. What they think. And why they think it. That's where the real world is, son."

Judge Anderson was right, of course. I'd spent most of my life growing up around similar kinds of people, but if you do not understand *all* people—people of varying backgrounds, socioeconomic statuses, religious beliefs, experiences, and thought processes—you will never be an effective communicator. If it's *real* people in the *real* world that you aspire to communicate with, move, and ultimately persuade, you've got to get better at understanding how they process information and the language that speaks to them particularly. You have to meet people where they are, not where you are and not where you may want them to be.

Learn how people think. Learn what motivates them. Learn what moves them. Learn what inspires them. Learn what scares them. Learn where they are. How they got there. And what it would take for them to move to something or somewhere else. You can lament the prejudices and preconceived notions others bring to conversations or you can accept certain near facts about human nature and begin to navigate them. What do people want? What do they crave? Where do they derive meaning and worth? Juries are a collection of jurors. Jurors are people and they bring all of their strengths and weaknesses into that courtroom with them. You better understand them if you are ever going to move them in any measurable way. That is true no matter where your jury is—inside or outside a courtroom. Be a student, a careful student of human nature.

By the way, Judge Ross Anderson, Jr., was everything I told you he was. He struck fear in the hearts of those who appeared before him. But he was more responsible for where I wound up in the legal profession than anyone else. He was a lifelong

Democrat who always used two words in front of the word "Republican" and one of those two words was "god." But the other was not. I don't like the words he used, so I asked him not to use them when I worked for him. And he stopped. At least while I was there. I love that man. He was complicated. He was mercurial. But if you were his, you were his forever. And the little bit I wound up knowing about human nature and how it impacts your ability to persuade I received from a lifelong Democrat who took the time to help a ***-**** Republican.

WHO'S YOUR JURY?

So, what do you know about your jury? What do you know about the individuals who comprise your jury?

Most of you will never stand in front of twelve of your fellow citizens in an attempt to persuade them in a criminal or civil case. But you will be surrounded by a jury of sorts for the rest of your life. It could be your family. It could be your bridge or poker partners. It could be friends at church, synagogue, or any other house of worship. It could be your shareholders. It could be your business partner, your customers, or those who want to someday soon be your customers. For you, the jury could be anyone you are trying to communicate with or move from one position to another.

The fact that you will not be in a courtroom does not mean you cannot learn from what happens there and the reasons we trust that process with some of the most important decisions in life. Think about it for a minute—from medical malpractice cases where an infant dies during childbirth to a homicide case where someone is facing either death or life in prison without parole, we trust the jury process. In business disputes, partnership dissolutions, libel cases, automobile wrecks, and insurance claims, we trust this thing we call a jury. So, it is worth knowing how the jury system works and what we can learn from it as we try our own hand at advocacy.

Chances are you have received or will receive a jury summons in the mail.

You show up at the courthouse and the judge begins to ask a series of questions to determine if you are even qualified to serve. What is your educational level? Can you read and write? Have you suffered a disqualifying criminal conviction? Do you know the lawyers, witnesses, or parties to the lawsuits or cases you may be asked to serve on? Do you know anything about the cases? Those would be the "facts" we discussed in the previous chapter. And even if you have heard some of the "facts," have you drawn conclusions from those facts? And even if you have drawn conclusions from those facts, can you set aside those previously held conclusions and have an open mind? Wow! That would be hard, wouldn't it? To set aside something you believe, think, or feel to be true and focus solely on what facts and evidence are presented in that particular trial. That is tantamount to a textbook definition of open-mindedness, isn't it? Starting fresh. Starting over. Wiping the slate clean and going right back to square neutral. Could you do that? Do you have the intellectual discipline to separate what you think you know from what you conclude is proven to you?

It's hard, isn't it? Despite my lifelong romance with cynicism about human nature, I was continually amazed by my fellow citizens and their ability to be objective and fair during this important part of a vitally important process. If you were the victim of domestic violence in the past, could you be fair and impartial in a domestic violence case? If you lost a child to a crib design or construction issue, could you be fair years later in a product liability case involving another child? Do you always believe certain witnesses or never believe certain witnesses? Are you biased for or against law enforcement? Could you set those preconceived beliefs aside and consider solely what came from the witness stand?

Our system requires us to find twelve people who can clean the slate, honor the presumption of innocence that attaches to the defendant, and be fair and impartial. But there is a misconception when it comes to voir dire. The reality is you do not "pick" a jury in court cases. You "unpick" a jury. Names are called and each side gets a certain number of strikes or exclusions. You cannot exercise your strikes based on race, gender, or age exclusively, but aside from certain legally protected categories you are trying to size up your fellow citizens to determine whether they would make good, fair jurors. You are not picking the jurors you most want to serve. You are excluding those that you do not want on that particular jury.

Assume there was a potential juror in the pool who had been accused of domestic violence eleven years ago but the charges were dismissed. Would you sit that juror in the domestic violence case you are about to prosecute? You need more facts, right? But you may not be getting any more facts. It's hard to size people up with only thirty minutes of exposure to them and a couple of pages of responses to boilerplate questions. But that is how juries are drawn, or picked, or, as you know now, "unpicked" in our justice system.

You are not likely to have the luxury of "unpicking" your jury. You cannot unpick a child or a co-worker or your sister's husband at Thanksgiving. You may well be stuck with a jury beyond your control, but that does not mean you cannot or should not use some of the same analytical tools to learn more about them. What is his or her background? Can you appeal to general fairness and open-mindedness? Can you agree on a larger, overarching principle and then begin to address the particulars? Isn't everyone opposed to mass shootings? Isn't everyone opposed to catastrophic medical bills that debilitate families and deplete savings? Isn't everyone supportive of a chance to attend college if that is what the young person wants to do? Isn't everyone in agreement that our criminal justice system should not punish children who have not even reached the legal age of accountability? You have just begun (slowly) a conversation or a response to some of the most volatile issues of our day: gun control, healthcare, student loan debt, and immigration.

This comes from being intentionally unprovocative on the front end while also sizing up the person with whom you are communicating and trying to understand where he or she is coming from and why.

I have a dear friend in Greenville, South Carolina, who is active in politics and a professor at a local university. She is conservative by any objective standard but she is not aggressive about it. She is genial. People like her. She is authentic. Early in my congressional days I would meet with the heads of the local conservative groups and Tea Parties. Contrary to popular mythology, I was not the Tea Party candidate in 2010. I did, however, host a lunch on immigration during a congressional recess so I could hear from them on the issue.

Various folks talked around the table with positions ranging from a far-right position to a more chamber-of-commerce position with a smattering of small-business owners in the construction and landscaping realms—all would be considered "conservative" positions on various points on the spectrum.

And then she spoke. She said her "mind had changed on immigration recently." We all sat up and paid close attention. In fact, she had made a complete 180. Wow! This is rare for a seasoned political operative and a professor. I wondered what happened? Did she read some treatise, some leading indicators on demographics and what the country needed to make up for the fact that we needed more workers? Did she talk to farmers in our district who, while conservative by any standard, were having a very hard time getting Americans to apply for and accept jobs picking peaches, strawberries, and blueberries? What happened? She's an academic. I couldn't wait to hear what changed her mind . . .

"I met a couple at church," she said. "They love this country, this is their home, albeit not lawfully, but I cannot support the displacing of this family."

That was it. This talented, smart, conservative thinker changed her mind based on a relationship. Not a book, or a political platform, or a candidate, but on a couple at her church.

Admittedly we cannot always base public policy on individual relationships or even our own personal experience. But it is illustrative of what it took to persuade her. And it is demonstrative of the fact that none of us at the lunch would have ever guessed it was a couple that changed her mind and not an argument or research.

We are all prisoners to a certain extent of what we have experienced, what we know ourselves, what we have seen in our own lives. You can get a sense of who and what your jury is only by listening to that. People are simultaneously complicated and simple. But our objective is to move these people, to communicate with them in hopes of eventual persuasion, and we do not have the luxury of "unpicking" our jury in real life, as we can in a courtroom. We should embrace the complexity and simplicity of the human experience, and that is best done by listening and trying to understand how someone got to where they are.

THE NEED FOR AN OPEN MIND

Death penalty juries are even more difficult to draw, because you have all of the issues we addressed above *plus* the additional question of what the proper punishment is if the defendant is found guilty of the underlying murder and the aggravating circumstances (which qualify the murder for the potential imposition of the death penalty). Aggravating circumstances are those additional factors that take a murder case to a capital murder case. Those factors differ state by state but typically include the fact that the murder was committed during the commission of another crime like burglary or robbery, the murder was committed against a child under a certain age, or the murder involved torture. The trials are bifurcated in South Carolina, which means the first trial is to determine whether the defendant committed the act of murder as it is legally defined in South Carolina. Then that trial goes all the way to verdict. If all twelve jurors unanimously conclude, beyond a reasonable doubt, that the defendant did, in fact, commit murder, they return a verdict indicting such. Then there is a twenty-four-hour "cooling off" period, and at the conclusion of that "cooling off" period a second trial begins to determine whether the proper punishment is death or life without parole.

The death penalty is a fascinating issue to debate and discuss in theory. As mentioned, I've changed my own mind on the issue a few times throughout my life. For most people it involves a mixture of public policy, spirituality, morality, economics, and levels of certainty. It's complicated and if the sentence is actually carried out, there is no appeal. I have seen a death sentence carried out. I've watched an execution. There is a double finality as the sentence is carried out. You are reminded of the finality of death from the victim's perspective and especially the perspective of the victim's family if they choose to attend. But you are also reminded of the finality of our own justice system for the convicted and the need to get it right—all of the time—because there is no appeal from the carrying out of a death sentence.

So in death penalty cases you question the jury pool just like you do in other kinds of criminal cases, but there is something additional that happens as well. Each juror is individually questioned by the judge and by the attorneys for the state or government and the attorneys for the defendant. It is just a citizen sitting in the witness chair being asked some of the most personal, probing questions you can be asked. Ordinarily those questions are none of anyone's business and certainly not the business of government. But this is not ordinary. This is to determine whether you are qualified to sit in judgment of a person in a case that may result in the state or federal government executing that person.

Jury selection begins with the potential juror sitting in the witness chair, nervous, unfamiliar with the process, about to be examined about very personal matters by a woman or a man in a black robe and then by total strangers with law degrees. Put yourself in the position of the judge. What would you ask? How would you start? The goal here is not persuasion. The goal is information. You do not care what the potential juror's position on the death penalty is at one level. You do care that that position be expressed and reliably so because you will be relying on the answers to these questions as you decide whom to "unpick" from the jury.

You would begin, perhaps, by putting the juror at ease. "Sir, or Madame, there is no right or wrong answer to the question I am about to ask you. We simply need an honest answer. Whatever the answer is, no one is going to try to convince you to adopt a different position. We simply need to know what your position is, okay? *What are your general thoughts and beliefs on the death penalty?*"

There are two kinds of jurors who are excluded from service in death penalty cases: those who would always give death and those who would always give life. If you believe taking a life results in the automatic forfeiting of your own, you are not eligible to serve in a death penalty case. Likewise, if you believe no one has the right to take a life, including the government, then you are not eligible to serve on a death penalty case. Frankly, that is a lot of people. People feel deeply on this matter and appropriately so. But that clean slate, that neutrality, that ability to say yes *and* no, is indispensable. If you cannot give death no matter how heinous the crime, how can you fairly sit on a case involving whether the death penalty should be the verdict? Similarly, if you believe that every life is the same and if you take one, you should give your own, then you have already made up your mind and do not have the objectivity needed for service in a death penalty case.

I learned a lot about people trying seven death penalty cases and spending countless hours interviewing people on what it is they believe and why it is they believe it.

The exchanges open a window into the human soul and how the mind processes beliefs, feelings, and facts.

PROSECUTOR: Sir, do you think you could give both life and death?

JUROR: Yes, I probably could, but I could not give death in, like, a theft case or a drug case.

PROSECUTOR: You do understand death would not even be an option in a theft case or a drug case, don't you? It would have to be a murder case with an aggravating circumstance.

JUROR: Oh, so this isn't giving death for stealing?

PROSECUTOR: No, sir, you can't give death for stealing. Sir, could you give both life and death, depending on what you believed was right and fair?

JUROR: No, I could only give death if a child were the victim. Like if someone killed my child.

PROSECUTOR: Sir, you do realize if someone killed your child you would not be on this jury?

JUROR: I wouldn't?

PROSECUTOR: No sir. You could not serve on a jury when it was your own family member that was the victim.

JUROR: Well, I could give it if someone else's child was killed.

PROSECUTOR: Only if the victim were a child?

JUROR: No, not really. I could give it maybe if the murder was not, like, in self-defense.

PROSECUTOR: Sir, you do realize you don't get the death penalty for killing someone in self-defense, don't you? Killing someone in self-defense is not even a crime, so there would be no guilty verdict and hence there would be no sentencing hearing for you to even consider punishment.

On and on and on it goes for days and days, trying to find jurors who could give both life and death depending on the facts. That is what we are trying to find. Open-minded citizens who wait and listen to the facts and then wait and decide on punishment. That is the process we go through in all cases with the extra process added in capital cases. But it certainly should make us appreciate the absolute necessity of having an open mind when it comes to persuading in general. It is hard, if not impossible, to persuade someone who is not persuadable. We have all had those conversations where you believed it would be more productive to go outside and argue with an oak tree. At least the tree would listen quietly.

EMPATHY'S INFLUENCE

There is a reason we encourage others not to judge unless and until they have walked a mile in someone else's shoes. There is a reason we are told people do not care how much you know, until they know how much you care. Clichés are clichés for a reason. They are true and time-tested.

The reason is that empathy is powerful. Empathy connects us. Empathy is a bridge you can traverse for the rest of your life.

Miranda Aull was a beautiful nineteen-year-old young woman strangled to death in 2002 by Jeremy Knight after she rebuffed his sexual advances. One of the hardest things you do as a prosecutor is meet with the family in the aftermath of a homicide. There really are no adequate words when parents lose a child, but the meeting between prosecutors and the surviving family members is important so the family can know what to expect in terms of the criminal justice process.

Miranda had two wonderful, loving parents. Her father, Eddie Aull, came to the courthouse for our initial meeting. And it was a short one. I don't even think Mr. Aull sat down. I will, however, never forget what he said before he left. He said he was "not sure a white man would assign value to a death of an African American young woman" and then he left. There were a half dozen prosecutors in our office capable of handling a homicide case, but when Mr. Aull left my office I decided to assign it to the one I knew would assign value to his daughter's life and in the process assign value to the grief he and his wife were feeling. I assigned it to myself.

Throughout that trial there were really two juries. There were the twelve women and men who would decide the case. That was one jury. Then there was the couple sitting in the first row behind the prosecutor's table watching the trial, watching the prosecutor, watching to see that our justice system assigned value to their precious child's life. That was an equally important jury to me. One jury had to be convinced beyond a reasonable doubt that Jeremy Knight murdered Miranda. The other jury? They just needed to be convinced that the justice system and its various components valued their daughter's life.

I saw Mr. Aull several years later in the parking lot of the post office. We embraced like friends. In 2019, Jeremy Knight was back in court trying to overturn the jury verdict and his sentence of life without parole. I've been to the courthouse only a couple of times since I left in December 2010. But I went back for this court hearing.

I did not go back to the Spartanburg County Courthouse because I was an indispensable witness in Jeremy Knight's post-conviction relief trial. I went back after all of these years because I wanted Eddie Aull to know I still value his daughter's life. Not as a prosecutor, because I am not one anymore, but as a father, because he and I will always be fathers to daughters, no matter how long ago a daughter has departed from us. I wanted Eddie to know that while I have no idea what it feels like to lose a daughter and pray I never know, I can be respectful of the fact that he experienced something that soul crushing and because it never will leave him, it should never leave me either.

There was a candlelight service for the victims of crime every December when I was a prosecutor. Our local sheriff and his team of victim advocates planned this event in order that those who lost loved ones could come together. And so I went. Sometimes I spoke; sometimes I did not. No one will ever recall a word I said. They will recall that I cared enough to go. There are no words for parents who lost a child to violence. There are no words for a husband who lost a wife to a drunk driver. There are no words for loved ones who have waited years and years for an arrest to be made in the case they live with on an hourly basis. People do not expect you to have the right thing to say. It is enough that you care enough to listen and be present.

So, sit down.
Listen to real people.
Know how they think.
Know what they think.
Know why they think it.
And then—if at all possible—feel what they feel.
That's where the real world is.

CHAPTER 5

THE BURDEN OF PROOF IS
IN THE PUDDING

DO YOU HAVE A SECOND?

By now you are well on your way toward identifying your objective, your purpose, your end goal. You also know (or are in
the process of gathering) all the relevant facts that undergird
your position, and you have spent some time considering the
other side of the issue or request. And you've done this for two
reasons: (1) It will make you better at communicating your own
objective, and (2) maybe there is wisdom in reflection and evaluation as it relates to our own position. You also have a clear
sense of whom, or which group, you are trying to move, persuade, or convince. In other words, you know who your jury is
and have spent some time evaluating their nature.

Now what?

Now comes the calibration. Now comes evaluating how
obtainable your objective is by determining how heavy a lift it
is. How convincing do you need to be? How much persuasion
is enough to move the person on the point you are trying to
make? Call it burden of proof. Call it evidentiary standard. Call

it "How good do I need to be?" Regardless of what you call it, the question comes down to: *How much evidence and advocacy will I need to win this discussion and accomplish my objective?* Marrying the burden of persuasion or burden of proof with your end objective is imperative for success. It is also intuitive for most of us. The larger the ask, the more convincing you need to be. The more contentious the issue, the better you need to be at persuasion. The smaller the ask or the smaller the issue, the more you can get away with fewer facts and less persuasion.

Sheria Akins Clarke was an investigative attorney on the House Ethics Committee when I first met her. The House Ethics Committee is the least desirable assignment in all of Congress, for members, that is. Not only are you investigating your colleagues for breaches of House Rules (not criminal conduct, mind you, but violations of the Rules of the House itself), but the assignment is very time consuming and completely confidential. In other words, you are in a room with a handful of other members for hours and when you emerge you cannot discuss any aspect of it with anyone who is not also on the House Ethics Committee. Not unlike the jury selection process we discussed, you are summoned for this assignment. You do not volunteer! So, when Speaker John Boehner sat beside me on the floor of the House one afternoon and said, "I need you to do something for me. I need you to serve on House Ethics," I agreed to it. If the Speaker of the House of Representatives asks you to do something, you have to do it. That's what I thought, at least.

Even if "no" had been an option, I would not have exercised it. Yes, it is hard and thankless. But it is also the least partisan, most apolitical committee in Congress. I like that. The members, on both sides, take the responsibility of fairly and justly investigating and adjudicating allegations of member misconduct seriously. When I think of Colorado governor Jared Polis,

I do not think of our many political differences; I think of our time together on the House Ethics Committee. So too with Anthony Brown from Maryland and Ted Deutch from Florida. Yes, all Democrats, and all thoughtful people I liked and respected. We can be as partisan as we want to be outside the committee room, but something refreshing took place when the doors were closed and fairness was the singular objective.

Reputations are on the line. The integrity of the House is on the line. Public confidence, admittedly at an all-time low as it relates to Congress, is also on the line.

It works like this. Someone on the investigative counsel, like Sheria Akins Clarke, would do the preliminary investigations for the committee and then present to the members by way of an oral report at our committee member meetings. The first time I heard Sheria speak at an Ethics Committee meeting, she was fact-centric, economical in her use of words, and anticipated most of the member questions before we asked them—all three really good qualities to have.

So, I did what I have done throughout most of my professional life: When I see a woman or man with a unique skill set, I make a mental note to keep that person in mind if the circumstances of life allow for an opening he or she might be qualified for. When Speaker Boehner asked me to lead the Select Committee on Events Surrounding the 2012 Terrorist Attack in Benghazi, Libya, I asked Sheria to join the investigation. When Congressman Jason Chaffetz left the chairmanship of the Committee on Oversight and Government Reform and I finished out his term, Sheria joined the committee as staff director. When I left Washington, DC, and headed back to South Carolina to practice law, Sheria, her husband, Jevon, and their three beautiful children came to South Carolina too.

There is one thing in particular that she is incredible at. Sheria is arguably the best in the world at intentionally misaligning the burden of proof with the objective. Correctly calibrating the burden of proof or evidence with the objective is imperative. Intentionally misaligning those two—in the way she does it—is even more effective.

"Trey, I have a really huge favor to ask. I'll understand if you cannot do it. I wish I did not even have to ask. I don't have anywhere else to turn."

That's a pretty typical introductory statement from Sheria.

So, of course you are thinking the same thing I am thinking. She is going to ask my wife and me to babysit their three children for a month while she and Jevon go to the Cayman Islands. Or, she is going to ask me to go see a nephrologist to determine if I am a match for a family member who needs a kidney transplant. Or, the biggest ask of all, she is going to ask to borrow my Odyssey #7 putter (which no one is even allowed to look at, much less touch or borrow).

But that is not what follows. What follows is usually "Can I borrow a pen? Mine stopped working." Or "Would you take a picture with an intern who is leaving today to head back to college?"

The predicate she lays is so out of sync and misaligned with the request that you are relieved at how small the request is and you immediately grant it. She overprepares you for the small request and your mind is so relieved at the small request that you grant it instinctively and immediately.

And we have all experienced the other side of that coin too, and it is devastatingly bad when it comes to trying to move someone or persuade someone.

I do the grocery shopping in our household almost every Saturday. My wife, a schoolteacher, works incredibly hard during the week, so it's something I can do to make her life easier.

Okay, that's not really the reason, but I felt better writing it.

The real reason is that she is the most beloved and popular person in our hometown, and it takes her hours and hours to get through the list because people are stopping her in every aisle of the store. There have been times when she placed a product in her cart and while she was still at the store, not even finished with her list, the product hits its expiration date! Not really, but it seems that way.

So, I do the shopping and from time to time I run into well-intentioned people whose calibration is completely out of sync between what they are seeking and what they can convince me of.

"Hey, Trey, do you have a second?"

What does "second" make you think? Easy question, easy answer, right?

"Sure," I say.

"What is the origin of evil and, if objective truth existed before one-third of the angels were expelled from heaven, what is the source of that objective evil they chose which led to their expulsion?"

"Umm . . . what did you just say? I am trying to read my wife's handwriting (artists have some loopy handwriting) and whether this version of Alfredo sauce exists anywhere other than in her mind—are you asking me a question that plagued great philosophers for centuries?"

Or perhaps the gentleman who asks you if you would mind attending their (not your) family reunion and giving them an update on what is happening in Washington?

"Well, I'm not sure I can. Where is your family reunion?"

"It's in Nebraska."

Those requests are not synchronized with reality. The burden of convincing someone to stop for "a second" in the grocery store and discuss the origin of evil or attend their family reunion one thousand miles away is incredibly high. And you are immediately aware that there is no correlation between what is being asked and the chances of your doing what is asked.

As a general rule of thumb, the smaller the ask, the smaller the amount of facts and persuasion is necessary; but the greater the ask—the greater the attempt to persuade or move someone from one position to another—the greater the quantum of proof and convincing.

In an unusual way, reflective of a part of human nature I am powerless to explain, Sheria's way of intentionally misaligning her ask with what is expected of me has a broader effect. I am conditioned to say "yes" when she asks for something. I am conditioned to appreciate her tacit acknowledgment that she is indeed asking for something. So that conditioning to say "yes" on little things makes me more likely to say "yes" on the larger requests. There is a belief, or a trust, if you will, that because she carefully calibrated what she asked for in the past, then whatever she asks for in the future would be similarly appropriately calibrated and therefore I should grant it. Being a good steward of the smaller requests makes her, at least in my mind, someone who can be trusted on the larger asks.

It's a little bit like what my father used to do when I was young. If he borrowed something, he returned it in better shape than he found it. If he borrowed someone's truck, he left it cleaner and with more gasoline than when he received it. If he borrowed a dollar, he paid you back at least a dollar and maybe more. It's akin to trust. People who have a real, genuine appreciation of what they are asking for are more likely to get the answer they want than someone who asks for a second and takes thirty minutes.

THE SLIDING SCALE OF BURDEN

What is most important to you? Which beliefs are most sacrosanct in your mind? For many of us it would be our spiritual or theological beliefs. So while we might reject a lecture from someone on their beliefs, or an attempt to proselytize, or maybe even reject an invitation to attend a house of worship other than our own, perhaps we are open to reading an article or attending a social event at that same house of worship. When you begin to communicate with someone on a new issue or an old one, you must have an internal tool of calibration that is constantly working and constantly adjusting. By that I mean you must appreciate exactly what you are asking that person to do and the significance of what you are asking. You must be respectful of the seriousness with which people hold certain convictions and beliefs. And if you sense you are asking for too much, immediately lower the request. It is far better to start small and incrementally work your way up. But sometimes we miss the mark. Perhaps we want someone to attend a meeting on a new product or a new financial opportunity. You would never ask for the investment first. You ask for an open mind, a willingness to listen.

Even the way we phrase our opening comments sets either the right or wrong tone. When you are asked, "Have you ever considered . . ." or "Are you open to hearing . . ." about an issue, you likely have a decidedly different reaction than if the person with whom you are communicating starts in a more declarative or dogmatic way, like a "you should" or "in reality." There is a reason I begin many sentences with "Are you open to . . . ?" No one considers herself or himself to be closed. So of course they want to be "open."

The burden of persuasion to get me to "consider" something or be "open" to something is much lower than getting me to accept or participate in something. That is true with most of us.

If it's important enough to you to bring it up, you can safely assume it is important enough to the person with whom you are communicating that he or she also has some firmly rooted convictions. If you are resolute in your own mind, chances are equally good that they are resolute in their own minds. So the correlation between what you are asking and the level of proof that will be expected to bridge the gap between request and acceptance must be close to exact.

Again, the criminal justice process proves helpful.

What does it take, from an evidentiary standpoint, for an officer to stop someone on the street and ask a question? Ever wondered that? What is required for a police officer to approach you and ask you a question? Not much, if anything. Officers are free to approach citizens and ask if that citizen has a minute.

So, too, in life we are welcome to approach friends, strangers, family, or co-workers. But we need to understand that our freedom to approach them is correspondent with their freedom to say "No, this is not a good time."

What about asking a motorist already stopped for a legitimate traffic infraction for permission to search the car? Again, very little evidence is required to ask, because the driver can say "no" and the inquiry usually ends there. That is called "consent." You can either consent or not consent, but there is next to no evidence required merely to ask. It's tantamount to asking someone if they are "open" to something or willing to "consider" something.

What about informing that same motorist that you smell marijuana and, while the motorist is free to go, you may call a canine to sniff the perimeter of the car for the presence of a controlled substance? How much evidence is required before an officer can call a canine to "search" the perimeter of your car by way of smell? The law calls it an "articulable suspicion." It's little more than a hunch, but not much more. There has to be some rationale for detaining the car, but you, the driver, are free to go. To be sure, you don't have a car to drive until the canine sniff is over, but you can at least in theory begin walking. On a scale of 0 to 100, it takes 0 to ask for consent to search. It takes 0 to ask a pedestrian if he or she has a second. It takes more, but not much more, to call a canine for the car. Keeping with our numerical scale, let's say it's 20 to 25 on a scale of 0 to 100 for what we call a level of proof equal to an "articulable suspicion."

What does it take to arrest someone? What does it take to obtain a search warrant from a judge to search a house or a business? It takes what the law calls "probable cause." That does not mean the person "probably did commit the crime" or evidence of a crime or contraband will "probably be there." Probable cause is more than a hunch but less than 50 percent sure. That's not a very high burden of proof, is it? Most of our fellow citizens would be surprised to learn you can be arrested or have your home searched based on a quantum of evidence less than 50 percent certainty. But that is the standard. On a scale of 0 to 100 percent, probable cause would be more than 35 percent but less than 50 percent.

Let's slide away from the criminal justice system and take a look at our civil justice system. As you may know, the civil justice system—while vitally important—is very distinct from the criminal realm. Think fighting for freedom when you think criminal. Think fighting for money when you think civil.

Contract disputes, automobile negligence cases, medical or legal malpractice cases, slip and fall cases, and premises liability cases are just some of the types of matters handled on the civil justice side of our justice system. Again, this civil side is very important, but very different.

One of the principal differences is in the burden of proof or burden of persuasion. In civil cases, you must convince the jury that something is more likely than not. We call it a "preponderance" of the evidence, but in its simplest terms it is whether any matter is more likely true than not true or more likely to have happened than not to have happened.

Some mistakenly believe that is equivalent to 51 percent on a scale of 1 to 100 percent, but it isn't. Even that is too high. It's 50.1 percent.

Imagine a set of scales that are perfectly level. Now in your mind put a feather or a string on one side of the scale. See that slight movement, ever so slight that it is barely discernible? That is a preponderance. It is not a particularly high level of proof or persuasion and it is quite eminently achievable in the real world. If you are trying to convince a co-worker to eat Italian rather than Mexican for lunch, preponderance will be enough to carry the day.

Occasionally in a courtroom you will run into a burden of proof called "clear and convincing" evidence. It's rare that you would need this level of persuasion in a courtroom, but it is commonplace that you would need it in real life, so it's worth addressing. Are you considering switching jobs? Are you considering whether to attend college in town or out of state? Are you considering whether to move residences, with all the headaches that accompany that decision? That feather or string we put on the scales of justice earlier would not and should not be enough to sway you. You need more than that. These are big decisions and the level of convincing—be it yourself or others—should be correspondingly large.

On the issues of significance that you are most likely to be discussing or attempting to persuade others on, this should be the realistic target to set in your own mind. Can you combine facts with an open-minded jury willing and capable of being moved, and convince someone that you are clearly correct? On a scale of 1 to 100 percent, 75 percent is "clear and convincing" and should more than meet your burden of proof.

The granddaddy of all evidentiary burdens is "beyond a reasonable doubt." You have heard that phrase a lot if you watch courtroom dramas or law-and-order shows. It is the burden required in all criminal cases. The question is, "What does 'beyond a reasonable doubt' mean and when and how do we achieve it?"—and that's a really good question that most attorneys would not even be able to explain to you.

In fact, in some courtrooms the attorneys are not even permitted to suggest or tell the jury what that phrase means. It's up to the judge to do that. But that doesn't help us much, does it? Especially if there is no judge present the next time you have Thanksgiving dinner with your family or in-laws and you sense an opportunity to communicate and convince. There are, thankfully, a couple of commonsense ways of looking at this evidentiary standard and how to understand it in its simplest terms. A reasonable doubt is a doubt that causes you to pause and consider not going forward on a serious issue in life. Perhaps I could convince you to invest $100 in a new start-up company. Nothing ventured, nothing gained. The risk is low if you are wrong. What if I asked you to invest $10,000 in that same company? That is going to require you to be more convinced, because the consequences of being wrong are more serious. What if I asked you to invest all the money you have worked so hard for and set aside for your children's education? How convinced would you need to be then? Pretty doggone convinced.

Now we are beginning to get a sense of what "beyond a reasonable doubt" is. Someone reading this chapter is going to say to herself or himself, even that is not enough for me to risk my children's college fund on. I want to be sure beyond *all* doubt. That is an impossible standard and because you cannot hope to meet it when it is your turn to convince, you should be careful not to require others to meet a standard you yourself could not meet.

You don't know everything there is to know about almost anything. So how could you possibly be convinced beyond all doubt? Part of persuading others is being open to being persuaded yourself, which means you are vigilantly on guard for any new fact or piece of evidence not previously considered. If there is always the potential for new facts and new evidence, then there is always the potential for some doubt. And hence, even when it comes to finding someone guilty of the most heinous crimes and imposing the most severe of all punishments, the standard of proof is not—because it cannot ever be—beyond all doubt. The doubt has to be reasonable. The doubt has to be one to which you can attach a reasoned, thoughtful apprehension.

So, what would cause you to pause in an important decision in life? That is the defensive way of looking at "beyond a reasonable doubt." The affirmative way of looking at it is, are you firmly convinced? Not merely convinced, but *firmly* convinced. On a scale of 1 to 100 percent, it would be 95 percent certitude in what you are saying or doing. It's high. It's exacting. It's as close to certainty as we are likely to come. And it's enough for the most serious crimes and the most serious punishments our society imposes. So if we reserve it for the most serious of matters in the criminal justice realm, it makes sense that we would reserve it for the most serious matters in life too, right? Whether or not to end a long relationship or friendship? Whether or not to marry someone? Whether or not to divorce someone? Whether or not to change religions? There will be few matters in life that require proof or evidence or persuasion beyond a reasonable doubt, but you should know what those matters are ahead of time, and adjust your level of proof accordingly.

Doubt is easy to create and hard to overcome. Keep that in mind as we continue the journey toward persuasion.

So be on the lookout when others sow the seeds of doubt about your own ideas and likewise be mindful of how to plant those seeds when you need to yourself.

One final observation on the burden of proof. While it never changes in the middle of a trial, it changes all the time in real life. Something that seems so small and trivial to us may be of supreme importance to the person with whom we are communicating. So, we need to readjust our level of persuasion, quite literally in the middle of the conversation. Some people have blind spots, pet peeves, and irrational fears or conceptions. We can lament the fact that they have those unusual areas where disproportionate levels of fact or evidence are needed to win the day, but that does not change the reality that a discussion that should be easy to have has morphed into something more. By listening and watching, whether it is an individual, a jury of twelve, the political opponent, or a conference room full of colleagues, we can sense that we need more; by sensing that need for more, we can adjust the sufficiency of our evidence to rise up and meet the level of persuasion.

So, remember that on your scale of burden of proof it goes as follows:

Consent: 0 percent

Articulable Suspicion: 20 to 25 percent

Probable Cause: 35 to 50 percent

Preponderance: 50.1 percent

Clear and Convincing: 75 percent

Beyond a Reasonable Doubt: 95 percent

Beyond All Doubt: Ha! Impossible.

But it leads me to ask: Why is it that in the modern political arena, we act as if our burden must fall on the outer edge of the spectrum for our opposition—beyond a reasonable doubt and, unreasonably, beyond all doubt? And, alternatively, falling at 0 percent evidence for those who agree and ratify our beliefs?

I cannot speak for all member experiences, but I can speak of my own while I was in Congress. I thought that the burden of persuasion—the amount of evidence needed for something like co-sponsoring a bill or working together on an important issue—would be pretty slight. It's just not that hard to find something two people agree on, even if they are on different ends of the political spectrum. Members have different views on the role of the federal government, the scope of that role, and how to implement those roles and scopes for sure, but surely there is *something* we can find that is worth pursing together.

The good news is that it happens more than you might think in Washington—the willingness to work together privately. The bad news is that it doesn't receive much attention (at least on the House side) because the political environment we currently find ourselves in makes the risks of that cooperation oftentimes outweigh the potential benefits of making that cooperation either significant or public. There were many Democrats I felt comfortable working with, despite our overall ideological differences, because they were honest in our interpersonal dealings; their motivations (as near I could tell) were public policy–driven and not politically driven. In my own experiences, those members included Tulsi Gabbard from Hawaii; Kyrsten Sinema, then a House member and now a senator from Arizona; Cedric Richmond from Louisiana; Zoe Lofgren from California; Hakeem Jeffries from New York; Peter Welch from Vermont; Kathleen Rice from New York; and Stacey Plaskett from the U.S. Virgin Islands.

But the member on the Democrat side that I talked to the most on legislative and policy matters was Joey Kennedy from Massachusetts. Joey and I are not likely to ever vote for each other; nor should we. We have different views on a number of issues. But he is hardworking, conscientious, earnest, and willing to listen. He is also passionate and well-informed on the issues closest to him. I would hire him in a skinny moment for any job that required integrity and perseverance and I hope he would consider me likewise.

In politics today, the burden of persuasion for convincing yourself that it is worth pursuing solutions across the aisle is harder than it used to be and harder than it should be. Almost everything in politics now requires proof beyond any doubt for our critics and little, if any, proof for our supporters. Hopefully, we can return to the days of the sliding scale where the heavy lifts require significant convincing and minds can remain open. Because everything should not be either an impossibly heavy lift or an empty scale.

CHAPTER 6

ONCE YOU LEARN TO FAKE SINCERITY, THERE IS NOTHING YOU CAN'T DO

THE UNIQUE POWERS OF AUTHENTICITY

Of the many pieces of advice Judge Ross Anderson gave me, one was the most simple: "Do everything David Stephens does in a courtroom."

You don't know David Stephens. He is a former state prosecutor and recently retired federal prosecutor in South Carolina. He's old school and worked his way up through the trenches in a way few do anymore. Trial after trial after trial. David lost more trials than most prosecutors will ever try—winning and losing combined. He is also the best litigator I have ever seen. Winning doesn't equal good. Good equals good, and David was the best. He was good because he was authentic. The juries believed him, the judges trusted him, and the defense counsel respected him.

Early in my career as a prosecutor, I tried to pick his brain on how to be an effective persuader and eventually I asked him to tell me the secret to being great in a courtroom. First, he mumbled something about how a carpenter has to be good with a hammer and a saw (translated: *You need to know the rules of evidence*). He mumbled something else about talking to real people (translated: *Enlarge the circle of people with whom you interact so you will be exposed to a cross section of the community*). Last, he mumbled something about sincerity and credibility. This one I heard loud and clear: "The secret to being a good communicator, Trey, is sincerity. Once you learn to fake that, there is nothing you cannot do."

I will remember that advice long after I forget my children's names or how far I hit a 7 iron. It's the single best advice you will ever get about effective communication and the hardest to perfect.

You cannot "fake" sincerity, of course, but I got what he meant. If you don't believe what you are saying, no one else will. If you are not invested in what you are selling, no one else will be either. If you are not passionate about what you believe, chances are the person with whom you are verbally sparring will not be, and passion is essential if you are engaging in passionate reasoning.

So, do you yourself believe what you claim to believe? Why do you believe it? How long have you believed it? What made you believe it? What options have you considered aside from believing it? Can you communicate what you believe in a convincing way, and if you cannot, what are the keys to learning how to communicate convincingly?

Emotions are important in the quest for sincerity. Emotions are best deployed to augment and complement other tools of persuasion—like facts, rationality, and logic—rather than as a stand-alone tool. But emotions are powerful and they work when it comes to moving people. The key to the most effective and long-lasting persuasion, however, is to go deep within the reserve of your sentiments and emotions and connect them to a larger precept or fundamental belief. Be emotional about fairness, be emotional about justice, be emotional about opportunity or education. Do not simply *be emotional*. To be effective, emotions cannot be engineered—they must be earnest—and the best way to have earnest emotion is to connect that emotion to some larger belief or truth. Manufactured or over-engineered emotions, on the other hand, are not only not helpful, they are destructive to what you are trying to accomplish.

We have all been present for the wedding or baby shower where the couple receives the twenty-seventh spatula or fifty-third box of baby wipes of the day. Their reaction makes you think they received the Hope Diamond. It's hard to act excited about a spatula or baby wipes, so while we may cut them some slack, it's hardly persuasive or believable.

So, what if you think something is important but you are having a hard time *feeling* it? How do you mirror the characteristics of realness on the days you don't feel all that invested in your topic? What about the days you believe something, but it's hard to conjure the passion? Well, that's most days, isn't it? We don't prearrange all of our efforts at communication or persuasion. We know going into Thanksgiving dinner that politics is likely to come up, but we don't necessarily plan on politics coming up in the parking lot of the mall.

David Stephens was not telling us to literally "fake sincerity," because you cannot, by definition, fake authenticity, and if you are suspected of trying to do so, your jury will judge you harshly. Ever hear the term "crocodile tears"? "Crocodile tears" is an expression we use when someone is faking real emotion, faking sincerity—faking empathy, compassion, or sorrow. The term comes from the ancient belief that crocodiles shed tears while they eat their prey. There's a reason we still use that term and it's not complimentary. Real emotion moves. Contrived emotion repels. When emotion is real, it is powerful. When emotion is contrived, it is destructive.

So, what did David Stephens mean? Simply this: Be sincere, genuine, and authentic as often as you can be. On those days when it is difficult to feel it fully, model the characteristics that are illustrative of sincerity. You are not "faking" with crocodile tears. You are, quite the opposite, so invested in the desire to model interest, empathy, and the ability to relate that you are willing to make the effort both consciously and subconsciously.

Without trying to sound like a Harlequin novel, it's a little bit like love. There are days when love is the most vivid emotion you have ever felt . . . and then there are days it is commitment regardless of how you happen to feel. But that doesn't discount love's existence, just because some days you've got to really work at it.

Similarly, I used to wonder how saleswomen and salesmen could be enthusiastic about selling suboptimal products. But maybe the guy selling a lower-grade vacuum cleaner isn't selling the vacuum cleaner at all. Maybe he's selling value. Maybe selling vacuums gives him more time with his family than his last job. Maybe a higher-grade vacuum ran over his dog's foot and hurt the little guy and the suboptimal vacuum could never cause so much suffering. If you are not feeling it about the vacuum itself, sell what you can get passionate about.

Passion in murder cases is not hard to conjure. Passion in crimes against children or vulnerable populations is not hard to experience. But everyday drug cases? How do you manage to be sincere, authentic, and credible about just another possession with intent to distribute controlled substances?

You find something *else* to be passionate about. Surely there is some fundamental precept you can latch on to.

David Stephens, in drug cases, would talk about an "evil wind sweeping across the playgrounds and schoolyards of

America, gathering lives in its wake." That was something he could be passionate and therefore sincere and authentic about. It was more than just another car stop on the interstate, with a canine car sniff, and a hidden compartment in the trunk full of cocaine. He had done a hundred of those. He found a principle, an ideal, or a precept he could consistently be sincere about. Eliciting an emotional response from a jury in a violent crime case is not difficult. Doing so in a drug case with no easily identifiable victim was much harder.

But what about expressing genuine emotion over a misdemeanor—a disturbing school case where a mom made a small scene and threw a temper tantrum? Come on. Who does that? The statutory maximum you can get for that is merely ninety days, for Pete's sake. It's hardly treason. Who would cry in a case like that?

I did! You can! You will! You will if you find a principle large enough to latch on to and an overarching precept bigger than that single moment.

THE PRINCIPLED PRINCIPAL

This was not a meeting I was looking forward to. An elementary school principal was stopping by the solicitor's office to discuss a disturbing school case that was very personal and important to her. The case went something like this: Robin Scruggs was dropping her child off at school one morning. Tardy. Again. The child walked through the office to sign in late and was greeted by an assistant principal. Ms. Scruggs claimed she saw the assistant principal strike the child and when she went into the school to confront the assistant principal, bedlam ensued. Scruggs was arrested for disturbing school and her defense was that the assistant principal struck her child and she acted in self-defense and defense of the child.

Ordinarily a disturbing-school case would never make it to my desk as solicitor. The two counties I represented as solicitor averaged between twenty and thirty homicides a year, scores of armed robberies, burglaries, domestic violence cases, and crimes against children. In fact, we averaged more than ten thousand warrants a year that needed to be processed and adjudicated through a system ill-equipped to handle numbers of warrants that large. So, no, I did not have time for a disturbing-school case. This particular case had been tried once before by someone else in the office and the jury was split 6-6. As you recall from earlier, criminal juries have to be unanimous. Losing six out of twelve jurors the first time around is not a harbinger for success in subsequent trials. Plus, the witnesses have already testified once and they are going to need to stick to what was said earlier. Nothing new or particularly probative is likely going to come from a second trial. It would be weeks of preparation for a trial that would take up a couple of days of already precious court time and the defendant wouldn't go to jail even if she was convicted. It just wasn't a good use of court time as I saw it. But the principal at Woodland Heights Elementary School saw it differently.

So we met.

And she won.

I lost.

Not only did I agree that our office would try the case again, I agreed that *I* would try the case again. Personally. Why? Authenticity. The principal brought the most persuasive piece of evidence she could possibly bring with her to our meeting: the assistant principal, whose impeccable career in public education was being tainted by the allegation that she would—or even could—strike a child. You could not listen to this assistant principal for any length of time without concluding that she was exactly the kind of person you would want to teach your own child or grandchild. Kind, gentle, nurturing, and unable to process how someone could accuse another person of striking a child in the absence of any proof. So, it was her authenticity that led me to take the case back to court. Her authenticity allowed the jury to see that no teacher or assistant principal (not this one, at least) is going to strike a small child for being late to school for the thirtieth plus time that semester. The child doesn't take himself to school. The child doesn't drive. The child isn't even old enough to walk or ride a bicycle to school. It is the parent's responsibility to get the child to school on time and this particular parent was terrible at that. Perhaps you would be tempted to smack the parent, but not the child.

The assistant principal's authenticity, sincerity, believability, and hence credibility inspired the others working on this case to locate their own internal emotional trigger. What would make you care enough to weep in front of strangers? Your own reputation. What would make you take a case for no logical reason? The right of a woman dedicated to teaching children to be heard and defended in the face of a serious accusation.

Yes, the assistant principal cried in court while she was testifying in front of the jury. So did I. She cried because she had been accused of the most insidious, destructive thing an educator could be accused of—hurting a child. I cried because I had come face-to-face with a type of purity of spirit not often seen. There was a purity in her belief that if we took the case to trial once more and the jury had a chance to hear it all, the right thing would be done.

And the right thing was done. The defendant was convicted. She had come into the school and made a scene not because her child was struck but because her child was tardy—again—and she needed something to obscure her own failure to get a child to school on time. The judge did not sentence her to jail or prison. What use would it have served? The child would have been the victim again. It's one thing to have a mother who habitually oversleeps. It's another to have a mother who is in prison for three months.

Authenticity can get people to do things they never would have considered doing. Authenticity can motivate, inspire, cajole, and persuade. I went from not taking the case at all to taking it myself. All in the course of half an hour. All because someone persuaded me that something was more important than my time. I went from laughing in my office at the mere idea of taking on a case that minor, to weeping in the courtroom because she persuaded me and reminded me of the things I believe in: fairness, honor, innocence.

While you may be stuck with the facts of whatever position you are trying to advocate for (in this case, a less-than-appealing school disturbance), there is no limit to the creativity of how you can fit those facts into the real lives of real people. If the issues are large, you do not need to do a thing other than state them fairly and simply. But on those days when you just don't feel especially passionate or sincere, remember what David Stephens said: Don't "fake" sincerity, because you cannot. Create something larger, appeal to a higher ideal, reach for a precept that is bold, and fit your arguments within that construct.

RULES OF ENGAGEMENT

Let's say you are just really, *really* not feeling it. I mean, your soul is empty, your heart is callous, and you are nihilistic beyond all human reason. (It's okay—we've all been there.) If you cannot be sincere—if you cannot be authentic—you can, at the very least, be engaged.

How do you do that, you ask? The same way you do it in other, more established relationships you value. You make eye contact. Your body language is welcoming, not repelling. You listen. You may not hear it all, but you are listening as best you can. We all have friends who repeat the same stories. Do you interrupt them and say "This is the same boring-as-Hades story you told me about your grandchild last week?" No, you act like it's the first time you have ever heard it. Why? Because it's engaging to listen and repelling to not.

Part of listening is asking follow-up questions. The more you are listening, the better the follow-up questions you will have, but there is a reason God created phrases like "Did you really?!," "That's amazing!," and "Then what happened?" You may not be listening intently but you are engaging intently and doing the best you can do.

The truth? I need to be better at this myself. There have been times when my dear, sweet, perfect wife has begun a story that had no beginning and no ending—like the story Hermes told Argus, at the direction of Zeus to circumvent Hera.* It began in one part of the house and ended at the other and I decided that retreating was the best option. Retreating in the face of a loved one's story is not engaging. Engaging is modeling the characteristics of real authenticity even when you do not feel it.

Luis Gutiérrez, the progressive former congressman from

---

* In this Greek myth, Zeus, who was married to Hera, fell in love with a young woman named Io. Before Hera could see Io, Zeus turned Io into a cow with the plan to turn her back into a beautiful woman as soon as Hera left and headed back home to Mount Olympus. But Hera was wise to his scheme and she commanded Argus to watch Io and make sure Zeus never completed this transformation from cow back to maiden. Argus had one hundred eyes, which meant he never slept. So Zeus sent Hermes to tell Argus a story that had no beginning and no ending, and slowly but surely each of those one hundred eyes fell asleep. Zeus then turned Io back into a beautiful maiden.

Illinois, put it perfectly: "People will vote for you if they do not like you; they will never vote for you if they think you do not like them." In other words, does the person with whom you are interacting believe that you are interested in him or her? Does the group you are speaking to believe you care about them and the topic you are discussing? This is being engaged.

Luis is right. People want to know you care about them. We like people who like us and we like people who are kind to us. I have seen it play out a thousand times in courtrooms and in politics. David Stephens would always compliment the defense attorneys in his opening statement to the jury. Why would you start off a trial by complimenting your opponent? Two reasons, actually: (1) The jury views you as a fair, neutral arbiter rather than just an advocate, and (2) it has an impact on the defense attorney. He or she feels compelled to respond to a compliment with a compliment.

In politics, we routinely hear politicians from different parties refer to others as "my friend from Texas" or "my friend from South Carolina." They do it even when they cannot stand the person they are calling "friend." Why? Because it works. It insulates you some from potential future criticism and you appear to be above the fray.

Part of being likable is understanding human nature and those characteristics most of us share. Remember, on balance, people would rather talk than listen. People tend to think conversations go better when they do most of the talking. We've all been in those situations where the person we were with did 90 percent of the talking and concluded, "I'm glad we had this talk. This was helpful." Once you learn—and, even more difficult, *accept*—that people would rather talk than listen, you can become a good listener. Not because it's easy or fun, but because it's productive in your efforts to persuade, and, as we will see later, it provides you with a treasure trove of information when you need to do proverbial battle with someone on an issue.

What else makes you likable? Conceding the small points. I've spent the better part of my life trying to get one of our two kids to clean her (that's a hint) room. She is a brilliant negotiator. She could solve the unrest in the Middle East if we sent her over there. She loves to bargain and negotiate and discuss. She doesn't love to clean her room (or bathroom) (or car). So, I will concede, "No, it doesn't have to be done by noon, it just has to be done by midnight; just sometime today, before it becomes tomorrow." I don't care when she cleans her room, just that she do so—or makes a small effort to do so. Almost every conversation presents you with opportunities to concede something: "I see what you are saying." "I understand where you are coming from." "I get why you believe what you believe." All of those make the same point: I am listening, I am considering what you say, and I am making an effort to understand and adapt.

Last, the way you structure your argument has a huge impact on whether you come off as likable, agreeable, and sincere or contentious, aggressive, and out for blood. Do you start with your most provocative point or do you start with your consensual point? I think it's best to start with a point that is nondebatable and then follow it up with one of your more fact-centric pieces of advocacy. For instance, people feel passionately on both sides of the issues that surround the Second Amendment and all people of good conscience are outraged at the epidemic of mass killings our country suffers from. I literally do not know a soul who is not moved to anger and tears when innocents are systematically gunned down with a weapon. The question is: What do we do about it, what will work, and what is consistent with other deeply held convictions about the right to self-defense? So, I treat this issue with sensitivity and respect for those with whom I may differ on the solutions. I begin my own advocacy by acknowledging what is obvious for me:

I spent close to two decades seeing firsthand the death, destruction, and pain wreaked by weapons used to take innocent lives. I spent the better part of two decades trying to stop people from killing other people and, when I failed at that, trying to help families get some small modicum of justice for their loved one. I know the controls we currently have on who can legally possess guns, what kinds of guns can be legally possessed, and where those guns can be legally possessed. That said, I am open to any idea you have to prevent innocents from being killed, so what additional controls would you propose and what is the data that leads you to believe that additional control would be effective?

In essence, assume that you can indeed *like* the person (or at least some aspect of the person) you are talking to and that you actually do have interest in what they are going to say and then voilà—you're already off to a great start to being likable and listened to in return.

WHATEVER YOU DO, DON'T DO THIS

We now know what works, but, as always, there is wisdom as well in understanding what does not work when it comes to persuasion.

The number one credibility killer when it comes to communicating your perspective to others is lying. "Lying" is a word that is used a lot in our culture, but it is used incorrectly most of the time. Lying is not simply making a false statement. There are scores of false statements uttered every day out of memory failures, innocent misrecollections, accidents, and mistakes. A false statement is the second-worst thing you can do if your goal is to communicate effectively or persuade, but it is not the worst. The worst is to make an *intentionally* false statement that is material to a point in question, with the intent to deceive. People can, will, and do forgive almost anything in life. But they are loath to forgive an effort to intentionally mislead them on an important and material point. What makes it even more insidious is the lingering effect it has on the listener. Let me loosely paraphrase Friedrich Nietzsche: *It's not that I am upset you lied to me, it is that I am upset I don't know when I can believe you in the future.* * Lying goes hand in hand with an inability to trust. That is true in relationships. It is true in business. It should be true in politics. But it is true in nearly every other facet of life. It is a persuasion killer, so do not lie.

False statements are not helpful, but at least you did not intend to deceive. Nonetheless, false factual pronouncements impeach your authenticity and call into question, and therefore jeopardize, the listener's ability to rely on you for the facts. It's survivable but damaging.

What else does not work if you are in the business of moving people from one point to another?

Insults don't work. I know you are disagreeing with me even as you read this because insults fill the airways, many said by people you may consider successful in business, politics, or entertainment. Insults are great at validating the convictions of your listener if your listener agrees with you in the first place. But you have no need to persuade those who already agree with you, do you? When was the last time you were motivated to reconsider a position because someone insulted you? When

---

* Friedrich Nietzsche, *Beyond Good and Evil* (New York: Vintage Books, 1966), Aphorism Number 183.

was the last time you liked someone right after they insulted you? What happens when we are insulted is that we become simultaneously defensive and aggressive. We are defensive of ourselves and desirous of repaying a slight with a better slight. What we tell ourselves and perhaps the person who insulted us is "I don't care what your facts are or how right you may be, I will go to my grave before I ever agree with what you just said." And oftentimes we mean it. We literally will never concede the point because we were insulted.

Truth be told, I can issue insults with the best of them. You cannot be in politics without knowing which buttons to push. And you cannot eat dinner with Mick Mulvaney, Tim Scott, Jason Chaffetz, Lindsey Graham, Marco Rubio, and John Ratcliffe without having thick skin and without knowing how to engage in verbal hand-to-hand combat.

Actually, you can eat lots of meals with Tim Scott with thin skin. Like I said, he is quite literally the kindest person in politics. But friends do pick on each other and my friends in Washington did it a lot. But that isn't persuasion (and those are not real insults). That is good-natured ribbing with some sharp edges from time to time. Insults are different, and while commonplace in politics and culture, they do not persuade anyone of anything.

Last, hypocrisy does not work. Duplicity does not work. Living by a separate set of rules than the ones you propose for others does not work. Persuasion requires movement. Hypocrisy, duplicity, relativism, and double standards do not lead to positive movement. They are useful tools if your objective is a full-fledged argument. Regrettably, life does afford those opportunities for full-fledged argument but, again, arguments succeed only in motivating those who already agree with you. That does not take very much skill. Persuasion requires skill and it's rare, which is why we call it an art.

By now you have learned to value the art of persuasion and have accepted and embraced the absolute necessity of knowing your facts, knowing who your jury is, and calibrating your objective with the appropriate burden of proof. You know the basics of what works (engagement, likability, and sincerity) and you know what doesn't (lying, insults, and hypocrisy). The groundwork's been done, the essentials are known, and the foundation is laid. Now it's time to move toward the act—the art—of persuasion itself. It's time to learn and utilize the indispensability of asking questions when it comes to accomplishing your communication goals. It's time to persuade those you speak with beyond their evidentiary threshold for movement, including, in some instances, beyond a reasonable doubt.

PART 2

THE ACT (AND ART)
OF PERSUASION

CHAPTER 7

CORROBORATE VS. CONTRADICT

THE SIXTY-FOUR-DOLLAR QUESTION ON THE FOURTH ESTATE

Imagine that you find yourself in the Oval Office with the leader of the free world on one side of the desk and representatives from the media on the other side and you are unexpectedly invited to join the conversation. This is likely to be a once-in-a-lifetime occurrence and you've got things to say! Points to make! Beliefs to share! What would you do? Are you confident enough in the power of questions to persuade and controlled enough to resist the temptation to speak in declaratives in your pursuit to persuade?

In early September 2019, I was in Washington, DC, for a meeting about a private law practice matter. At the time, I was no longer in Congress, so I rarely had any reason to be in DC anymore. The House and the Senate were not yet back in session after the August recess, so there was no need to alert my friends in those two bodies that I was in town. But I knew my former colleague and dinner companion Mick Mulvaney was in DC, so I sent him a quick text letting him know I was there, had a flight back to South Carolina midafternoon, and I didn't need or want a thing except to let him know I had come and gone. "Come by for lunch on your way back to the airport" was his response.

Like an idiot, I took my tie off on the ride to the White House. Moments after entering the lobby I heard Mick yell, "Go get Trey a tie! I'm going to walk him in to say hello to the boss."

The boss? Let me think for a second. Mick is chief of staff for the president of the United States. Is that what he means by the "boss"?

"Umm Mick, I would have gotten a haircut if I had known I was going to be seeing the president," I said.

"What difference would that make?" he responded. "It looks equally bad long or short."

Hurricane Dorian was on the verge of hitting the Bahamas and for reasons I probably won't ever fully understand, the headlines were dominated by whether or not the president had included Alabama in the states potentially impacted by the storm. In a nutshell, when mentioning states that would likely be impacted by the storm in a tweet, he included Alabama, which by then was reported not to be under threat from the storm. (I'll lay aside for the moment our culture's hyperfixation with negativity as well as our culture's reluctance to admit that mistakes do indeed exist and when we, in fact, make those mistakes.)

What I walked into was a conversation in the Oval Office between President Trump and representatives of the media about fairness, completeness, objectivity, and bias, all discussed against the backdrop of a need for and an acknowledged desire for a robust, free, and respected Fourth Estate.

I had not been present at the side of the president's desk for more than ten seconds before he asked me to weigh in with my perspective on the issues he was discussing with the representatives of the media.

What would you do? What would be the next words out of your mouth? It's an important conversation. It's a necessary conversation in our current political and cultural environment. It was an unexpected conversation for sure. I did not wake up in South Carolina early that morning expecting to be in the Oval Office observing a conversation about media standards and fundamental fairness against the backdrop of a hurricane.

Having been in politics for nearly two decades, with the last eight years in Washington forming my own perspective on the media and how it interacts with elected officials and others in positions of responsibility, I certainly had an opinion. But I did not state it. I did what I would encourage you to do: I asked a question. And then another question. And then another question. I did not ask questions because I needed more information. I did not ask questions because I wasn't sure of the facts. I asked questions because, in that moment, I was convinced that asking questions carried the greater likelihood of persuasion than simply stating declarative sentences that began "I believe," "I think," or "I feel."

I am not going to repeat what the president said or what any members of the media said. Not because it's classified and not because anyone asked me to keep the conversation to myself. No one said, "What happens in here stays in here." It's just my own internal sense of fairness that dictates that, under these facts, invited guests do not relay private conversations.

But I will tell you what *I* said. First, I asked, "Why is our justice system more respected than our political system? Why is there something called a rule of completeness in our justice system? If it's enough for that system we respect, why not try it with other institutions? If I said 'Mick pulled a gun on me' but

I failed to include the fact that 'I pulled a gun on him first,' is that fair? What is the tool we use most in life to elucidate the truth?"

While you may not find yourself in the middle of an animated, though important, conversation in the Oval Office between the president of the United States and members of the media, chances are you *will* find yourself either inserted into or being brought into a conversation of significance and importance.

Would you consider your opening utterance being a question? Of course you would if you were trying to gather more information. But what if you were beyond the fact-gathering stage and on to the persuasion stage? Do you now trust in the power of questions enough to start there rather than "Let me tell you what I think"? Because that is the temptation, right? When others trust you enough to bring you in to participate in or referee a conversation, the temptation is to wow them with some pearl of wisdom or truth.

What I wanted to do in the Oval Office is persuade by crystallizing and distilling the issues away from the political environment and on to an environment exponentially more respected. And while, sure, *sometimes* lectures work, questions almost *always* work—especially when the questions incorporate the issues at hand and frame those issues in the way you desire.

When it comes to the art of persuasion, there are only two objectives with your questions. That's not too hard, is it? Two objectives for any and all questions asked. We can do this!

Questions either (1) corroborate or (2) contradict. They either advance your own point or slow down the other person's point. Questions tend to either prove or disprove the point in contention. Questions make the point at hand more or less likely to be true.

Take the questions I asked in the Oval Office. Do you really think I was asking members of the media for an analysis of the justice system? Of course not. My point was that the justice system is more respected than either politics or the media because completeness, and therefore fairness, is embedded in the system—and it is embedded precisely because completeness and fairness are coupled. There is a rule of completeness in our justice system, so why not have one in other important facets, like politics and reporting too?

Use the example of Mick and me pulling a gun. (And for those who need to be reassured: No, Mick and I have never pulled guns or any other kind of weapon on each other. Although, if he has forty-three putts in eighteen holes as he did once as my partner in a golf match, I reserve the right to revisit this issue.) It is accurate, in my hypothetical, to say, "Mick pulled a gun on me." In my imaginary fact pattern, that statement is true. It is also manifestly unfair to simply state that fact without also mentioning that he did it in self-defense. There is no word limit in a courtroom. We are not reduced to fitting our evidence into a certain number of characters in a tweet. We are not on a deadline in a courtroom. We are not trying to become famous in a courtroom. There is no pressure to create headlines so the public will click on a certain story, and we are roundly punished by both the judge and the jury if we intentionally omit relevant facts that put other facts in context.

That's the broader point. People of good conscience would universally concede that leaving out a fact as important as brandishing a weapon in self-defense is unfair, lacks credibility, and otherwise undercuts the objectivity of the person leaving out said fact.

Asking the questions I did, in the way I did it, was calculated to make points of corroboration and contradiction without overtly doing so.

Why do we have a rule of completeness in the justice system? Because completeness is what we should all strive for if fairness is part of the process. It may well be true that the president mentioned Alabama. So, it is true to say he did so. It's just unfair to leave the reader or listener with the impression that that is the *only* state he mentioned (he mentioned South Carolina, North Carolina, and Georgia, which were indeed threatened by the storm). You can also effectively question the interest or motive of someone who paid a disproportionate level of attention to Alabama to the exclusion or minimization of other states. What is lost by journalists *also* mentioning the other three states when telling the story of what is now known as the Hurricane Dorian–Alabama Controversy? Why not state *all* the facts? What is gained by emphasizing the president's inclusion of Alabama while deemphasizing his inclusion of other states? If your objective is to belittle the president for including Alabama, couldn't you still do that by giving the whole truth of what was said? My question was designed to contradict the media's protestations that accuracy is de facto fairness. You can be both accurate and unfair, but it's actually *easier* to be both accurate and fair if you are also complete. More folks ought to try it.

I did not seek or even desire to be inserted into the president's conversation with the media that afternoon. But once inserted, the way to make the points I believed most salient was by using questions calculated to corroborate or contradict. Your questions should have a point—whether overt or covert, obvious or subtle, nuanced or coarse—but a point nonetheless. As it relates to persuasion and proving or disproving positions, the two points at your disposal are to build up or tear down, advance or retreat, corroborate or contradict.

SOFTBALL AND HARDBALL

As a kid, I loved all sports but *especially* baseball. Like most little boys, waiting for my father to pull into the driveway after work is one of my most vivid, recurring memories from childhood. I later came to realize daddies are tired after work. They actually want to change clothes and relax for a second before going in the backyard and throwing the baseball (but it took becoming a father to appreciate that). As a kid, I had both of our gloves ready to throw the baseball as soon as he got out of his car—dress clothes and all.

My father could throw the highest pop flies, and I would camp under the ball and nervously wait for it to hopefully find my glove. Many times it did find my glove—sometimes it found my head—and while my father was a pediatrician and understood that getting hit in the forehead with a baseball glancing off a glove would likely not kill me, my mother did not understand that. So, she lovingly encouraged me to either find a new sport or get a metal plate inserted in my forehead.

Instead, I decided to learn to catch. I would lie on my back in the den and throw a ball up near the ceiling and catch it before it hit my head. But a real baseball would have been too tough a teacher. So, I began to throw a tennis ball. There is a huge difference between getting hit in the head by a tennis ball and a baseball, and if you have ever been hit in the head with both you can appreciate the difference between hard and soft.

Have you ever heard the phrase "softball question"? A "softball question" is an easy question; a "hardball question" is a difficult question. Softball questions corroborate; for example, at a White House press conference, a reporter might ask, *Mr. President, did you enjoy your Labor Day weekend?* That's a softball question.

It's like being in a job interview and being asked what your greatest strength is. It's a question designed to be easy so as to allow the person answering to make a point or advance a position. It's an invitation to persuade.

We have all seen these types of questions in political debates; questions that maybe the candidate himself or herself wrote. *Why are you running for office? What makes you the most qualified candidate? How does it feel to be so wonderful? Do you ever get tired of being perfect?* Those are softball questions and they are designed to credit, corroborate, or advance a position or a person.

In a banking sense, those questions allow you to make deposits in the credibility, believability, or likability accounts. And, as we've learned, those three traits—credibility, believability, and likability—are integral to persuasion.

The other type of question contradicts, undercuts, or impeaches. These are hardball questions. It makes withdrawals from those same three accounts: credibility, believability, and likability. *What did you mean by "no new taxes" when you raised them three times as governor? When did you stop drinking on the job? How can you get above 0.0 in the polls?* These questions undercut, they impeach, and they tend to cast the person answering in a defensive or negative light.

The same goes when you're in the courtroom. You are either asking them to build something (corroborate) or asking them to tear something or someone down (contradict). And sometimes the exact same question can be used to both contradict and corroborate. It just depends on the motive or purpose behind who is doing it and when it is done.

In your own life, you will have a sense of whether someone is with you or against you. Whether it is a political issue or whether it is finding a soulmate who also pulls for the Dallas Cowboys, you get a sense pretty early on in most conversations as to whether someone is a friend or a foe—at least on the particular issue at hand.

You will know this not only by the content of their questions and answers but also the tone and the texture of their response. So, with friends and allies your objective is (hopefully) to corroborate, to build up. Give them opportunities to expound. Give them facts embedded in your question that buttress your position. *When Dallas won back-to-back Super Bowls, how old were you? Which Super Bowl victory was it when Jimmy Johnson yelled "How 'bout them Cowboys?" How far ahead were we when Leon Lett got caught from behind as he was about to score a defensive touchdown?* Those are all friendly questions designed to make several points—mainly that Dallas is great and won some Super Bowls, including one by a large margin over the Buffalo Bills.

Now, what if you—heaven forbid—are not a Dallas Cowboy fan? First, repent and ask forgiveness. Then, if that doesn't work and you still want to impeach or contradict someone talking pro football, your questions would be very different, right? *Was the Revolutionary War over when Dallas won its last Super Bowl? Were the helmets made of leather? Had leather even been invented when Dallas last won the Super Bowl?* Those are not friendly questions and, to be honest, I did not even enjoy writing them.

LOVE AND PRISON

Some questions can go either or both ways. The question may be the same but the intent is decidedly different.

Sonya Pabellon was the wife of Tommy Pabellon. Tommy Pabellon was charged with the murder of a federal witness in South Carolina. When the police first talked with Sonya Pabellon about what she knew about the incident, she was far less than honest. She claimed she didn't know anything, hadn't heard anything, and generally had no idea what she was being asked. She wasn't convincing but she was consistent.

There is nothing quite like being arrested by federal law enforcement agents to refresh one's recollection. Sonya was arrested on separate drug charges, and the police talked to her again concerning what she knew about the murder of this federal witness and her husband's involvement. This time her memory was better.

If you are the prosecutor and Sonya is an important witness to your case, you need to address her prior statements (where she denied knowledge) while keeping in mind that you have a very different purpose and objective than if you were the defense attorney trying to impeach her.

As a prosecutor, when you ask her on the witness stand, "Why did you lie to the police when they interviewed you the first time?" that is a question designed to allow her a chance to explain. It is a question designed to corroborate her testimony by allowing her to admit she did in fact lie the first time around and to explain why. It is designed to make her more believable because it gives her a chance to acknowledge that she was intentionally wrong the first time she was asked. While it is a negative fact that must be addressed, your purpose in asking the question is to make her appear more credible. Volunteering negative information oftentimes casts the volunteer in a more favorable light.

After denying her husband had any involvement with the murder of a federal witness and after she was arrested on her own drug charges, Sonya Pabellon was interviewed by the police again. This time, in her second police interview, she told the police that her husband was indeed involved in the murder of a federal witness. When the defense counsel asked Ms. Pabellon why she lied when she talked with the police the second time they interviewed her and implicated her husband, that was an effort to contradict her, to impeach her, to make her testimony less likely to be believed.

It's the same question—"Why did you lie?"—but with two different expectations and opportunities.

By the way, Ms. Pabellon's answer was about as good as it could be for a question like "Why did you lie?" She testified and said, "When it was between my husband and the police, I chose my husband. When it was between my husband and me, I chose the truth." The jury believed her. Tommy Pabellon was convicted and is serving four life sentences without the possibility of parole in the Federal Bureau of Prisons.

In life, there are a limitless number of reasons why we ask questions. Sometimes we really do need to know what time it is. Sometimes we really are interested in whether someone liked *The English Patient.* Sometimes we really are trying to gain knowledge on an issue like why Jason Garrett, the former coach of my beloved Dallas Cowboys, loves field goals more than I love my children. See there, I can't stop! That last question is not a desire for more information. It is designed to persuade Coach Garrett to go for it more on fourth and one in the red zone.

But as it relates to persuasion, there is only one of two purposes in asking questions and essentially only these two: corroborate or contradict. There are those that add or those that subtract, those that make deposits into the accounts we value or those that make withdrawals, those that get us closer to our target or those that impede and obstruct others in their pursuit of their target.

So, now that we know the two *purposes or objectives* in asking questions, we can move on to the two and a half *types* of questions. But worry not. I failed math, remember? This is about as mathematical as we'll get, I swear.

CHAPTER 8

LEADING AND NON-LEADING THE WAY

TWO AND A HALF WAYS TO GET THERE

Welcome to court!

RULE 611. MODE AND ORDER OF EXAMINING WITNESSES AND PRESENTING EVIDENCE

(a) **Control by the Court; Purposes.** The court should exercise reasonable control over the mode and order of examining witnesses and presenting evidence so as to:

(1) make those procedures effective for determining the truth;

(2) avoid wasting time; and

(3) protect witnesses from harassment or undue embarrassment.

(b) **Scope of Cross-Examination.** Cross-examination should not go beyond the subject matter of the direct examination and matters affecting the witness's credibility. The court may allow inquiry into additional matters as if on direct examination.

(c) **Leading Questions.** Leading questions should not be used on direct examination except as necessary to develop the witness's testimony. Ordinarily, the court should allow leading questions:

(1) on cross-examination; and

(2) when a party calls a hostile witness, an adverse party, or a witness identified with an adverse party.

This is the evidentiary rule that governs the manner of questioning witnesses in court. You will note section (c) is entitled "Leading Questions," and leading questions may not be used on direct examination in a courtroom. Direct examination in general terms is when you are asking questions of a witness you have called. In a medical malpractice case, if you are the plaintiff's attorney, it is you calling the person who was the patient and is alleging malpractice. In a criminal case, if you are the prosecutor, it is you calling the bank teller who was present when someone in a ski mask came in and handed her a demand note. That is direct examination and leading questions are not allowed, ordinarily.

The opposite of direct examination is what we call cross-examination. Cross-examination receives a disproportionate amount of attention. Television shows and movies rarely show dramatic scenes of direct examination. It is the cross-examination by a prosecutor of a defendant or the cross-examination of a victim by defense counsel that garners more attention than the direct examination of a witness by his or her own attorney. But do not be fooled by that. Direct examination is where the story is told. Direct examination is where the information is imparted. Direct examination, more often than not, is where cases are actually won and lost.

In the last chapter, we learned that there are two *purposes* when asking questions: (1) to corroborate and (2) to contradict.

In this chapter, we'll focus on the two and a half *types* of questions—at least as it relates to moving people from one position to another. In life, as it relates to communication and persuasion, there are those two principal types of questions—non-leading and leading—but we are going to add a (nearly) third category. They are the "half" and they are the "why" questions.

NON-LEADING QUESTIONS

A non-leading question is what we think of when we think of questions in everyday life. These are questions that usually begin with "who," "what," "when," "where," and "how." These are questions that seek information (and are what we use in direct examination).

What time is it?

Who was the last person in the office?

When did you leave for vacation?

Where did you leave my book?

The focus is on the answer and not on the question. If you are in court and have the burden of proof as either a prosecutor or a plaintiff, non-leading questions are what you ask of your witnesses. Non-leading questions can be smart, they can be effective, and they can be illuminating. But they do not suggest what the answer should be, as leading questions do.

Prosecutors are oftentimes more known for their cross-examinations of defendants than their direct examinations of witnesses and victims. But it is these direct examinations, using non-leading questions, that make the case. Non-leading questions allow you to present affirmatively and proactively rather than the reactionary nature of leading questions.

In death penalty cases, for instance, you will use non-leading questions to give the jury a sense of the loss the victim's family feels.

What is the last thing you said to your daughter before she was killed?

What do you miss most about your mother?

What kind of person was your brother?

How would you describe your sister's relationship with her children? What kind of mother was she?

If you could talk to your father one last time, what would you like to say to him?

In life, we use non-leading questions most of the time.

Who do we want to invite over for dinner?

What do you want to do today, honey?

When do we want to go to the grocery store this week?

Where did you get that awesome tie?

How was your day at school?

There are several upsides to non-leading questions, including (1) you are likely to build a better rapport with the person you are asking questions of, (2) you are less likely to offend because of the open-endedness of the question, and (3) you allow the person to make his or her point in an uninterrupted way.

The downside to using non-leading questions is that you have lost some control in steering the direction of the conversation.

Lindsey Graham's first encounter with Joe Biden proves this point.

As Lindsey tells the story, he was new to the Senate and was going on a CODEL (congressional delegation) with Joe Biden. Graham did not know Biden well at the time, and they had a fourteen-hour flight ahead of them seated beside each other. So, as they were taking off from Andrews Air Force Base, Lindsey turned to Biden and asked, "What's happening with Delaware politics these days?" According to Lindsey as the plane was landing in Baghdad, Biden turned to him and said, "I'll finish the story in the cab on the way to the hotel!"

I doubt (sort of) that Biden talked for fourteen straight hours about Delaware politics. But Lindsey's story is funny and illustrative of the power and limitations of non-leading questions. You get the person to talk but sometimes they talk a lot and by the time they stop talking, you forget what you asked originally.

LEADING QUESTIONS

One of my great frustrations with congressional hearings was the artificial time limit within which you expect members or witnesses to make significant progress. Can you think of any other facet of life where you acknowledge that the issues are important and oftentimes complex, yet you limit the discussion of those issues to only five minutes? Which is why, in Congress, you almost never see non-leading questions used in hearings. That's not because these questions aren't effective; it's because of the five-minute time limit, which impedes anyone's ability to effectively make much of a point.

When you are constantly worrying about running out of time or worrying about a witness taking too long to answer one question when you have three more you would like to ask, it almost forces you to use leading questions just to hurry the process along.

Therefore, what you see in congressional hearings, in courtrooms during cross-examination, and frequently on television talk shows is *leading questions*. These leading questions suggest the answer, put the focus on the person asking the question rather than the person answering, and are oftentimes more confrontational.

> *"Isn't it true I told you to clean up your room six times?"*
>
> *"You came in over an hour and a half late last night, didn't you?*
>
> *"Didn't you take the last cup of coffee and fail to make any more?"*
>
> *"Isn't it a fact you were late to work today?"*

In the talk show context, it unfortunately goes something like this: *You voted against additional funding for program XYZ—do you really hate children that much?* or *The Department of State is full of deep state actors hell-bent on bringing this administration down, isn't it?*

Those are all leading questions. They essentially state an assertion and leave you with the option of assenting to or dissenting from that assertion. These questions are designed to pin someone down, force someone to admit a fact or concede a point. The questioner is in total control. These leading types of questions are almost inherently argumentative. In a courtroom these types of questions are reserved for cross-examination of witnesses or, in the case where even a witness you called to the stand is being hostile, uncooperative, or perhaps even too frightened to carry the load of testifying, so you essentially testify *for* them by stating a fact and saying, *Isn't that so?*

Leading questions can also be helpful when you are trying to assist a witness who is struggling.

This book is not about politics or telling you what you should believe. But my experiences with questions—and therefore my illustrations about using questions—necessarily come from either the courtroom, Congress, or my own life.

I say that because I do not want you to focus on the substance of my questions or the substance of the answers in any illustrations I provide. You are welcome to form whatever opinion you want to form about any political issue! If I enjoyed politics personally, I would not have left. I do not use examples from congressional investigations or hearings because I enjoy politics but rather because over my eight years in Congress, I was able to ask questions of some well-known, smart, and savvy people like Secretary Hillary Clinton, former secretary of defense Leon Panetta, former CIA director David Petraeus, former FBI director James Comey, U.S. Senator Elizabeth Warren, former attorney general Eric Holder, Jared Kushner, Inspector General Michael Horowitz, Samantha Power, Ben Rhodes, and Susan Rice. Off camera I had a chance to visit with and ask questions of the lead singer of the world's greatest rock band, Bono from U2; brilliant legal minds like Paul Clement; and what will always be the most difficult day of all in public service, the day Speaker John Boehner asked me to join him in meeting with the parents of children murdered at Sandy Hook Elementary School.

In the examples I provide, some of you will agree with my questions and some of you will not. Some of you will side with the person answering the questions and some of you will not. None of that is any of my business, and your political ideations, if any, are of no consequence when it comes to using questions to make your case. But I can draw only on my experiences when making my case. So please bear with me.

While I was on the House Permanent Select Committee on Intelligence, I was asked to interview dozens of witnesses related to Russian interference in our election, allegations of collusion with the Russian government, as well as issues related to our own government's response. One of those witnesses was former attorney general Jeff Sessions and one of the areas of inquiry was the now famous email string between Donald Trump, Jr., and Rob Goldstone setting up the meeting at Trump Tower in June 2016.

Jeff Sessions is certainly a smart, capable person. You don't become a United States attorney, a United States senator, and the attorney general for the United States without being capable. But this was going to be a difficult interview for him for a variety of reasons. And unlike a courtroom or even a public interview, there was no jury of our fellow citizens present to make sure the questions were fair and the process was reasonable. So, what would you do? There were sure to be very difficult topics to address, such as his recusal from the Russia investigation, his support of then candidate Trump, and his testimony before the Senate Judiciary Committee during his confirmation hearing. How would you handle these various issues at hand during this interview? This interview would be primarily about the Russia investigation, so the email between Rob Goldstone and Donald Trump, Jr., would be emphasized.

Here is the first in the email string and the one that generated the most questions:

June 3, 2016, at 10:36 AM, Rob Goldstone wrote to Donald Trump, Jr.:

Good morning
Emin just called and asked me to contact you with something very interesting.

The Crown prosecutor of Russia met with his father Aras this morning and in their meeting offered to provide the Trump campaign with some official documents and information that would incriminate Hillary and her dealings with Russia and would be very useful to your father.

This is obviously very high level and sensitive infor-

mation but is part of Russia and its government's support
for Mr. Trump—helped along by Aras and Emin.

What do you think is the best way to handle this information and would you be able to speak to Emin
about it directly?

I can also send this info to your father via Rhona, but
it is ultra sensitive so wanted to send to you first.

Best

Rob Goldstone

I decided to use leading questions with Attorney General
Sessions, not because he was not capable of answering non-
leading ones but because there were certain points to be made
and those points were best made using leading questions. I did
not use leading questions because of any time limits. Unlike
other congressional hearings, there were no time constraints
during these interviews. But I did perceive a need to direct the
lines of inquiry and to highlight certain matters in a certain
order, and leading questions were far more likely to be effective
than non-leading ones.

Obviously, you would start by highlighting the reality that
there is no Crown prosecutor of Russia, right? That does not
mean the rest of the email is fundamentally flawed, but we will
remember well from earlier chapters that factual errors do undercut the reliability of what comes thereafter. And, of course,
you will keep in mind that this email is tantamount to a notice
email. By that I mean House Democrats would use the email to
show that the participants knew full well and therefore were on
notice that the meeting was not about the adoption of Russian
children (per the statement issued by Donald Trump, Jr.) but
rather was about gathering information from a Russian lawyer
about Secretary Clinton. You cannot avoid that fact, so you
must confront it and do so directly.

What you would want to do with Attorney General Sessions is take the most damning line from this email and confront it directly using leading questions, with that line being: "offered to provide the Trump campaign with some official documents and information that would incriminate Hillary and her dealings with Russia and would be very useful to your father."

While it's not an exact transcript, this is what I intended to ask, did ask in some instances, or wish I had asked in hindsight:

"Secretary Clinton had been First Lady, a United States senator, and secretary of state, right?"

"Two of those jobs for certain and perhaps all three would have generated documents, right?"

"Those documents would have been official documents, right?"

"The email says, 'official documents and information,' doesn't it?"

"Not personal information, right?"

"Nothing about emails or personal information, correct?"

"If it's official, it's already in the public domain, isn't it?"

"The word 'official' can modify both the words 'documents' and 'information,' right?"

"So, is that what the issue is, that someone offered to provide official information from her time as a public figure working in or on behalf of the U.S. government? Is that what this is about?"

"Official is already *official,* isn't it?"

"She had 'dealings with Russia' as a senator, right?"

"*Could have,* right?"

"*Definitely* had dealings with Russia as secretary of state, right?"

"So, the Russians are offering to tell us what her official dealings were with Russia when she was officially our emissary to them?"

"We'd already know that, wouldn't we?"

"Let me make sure I have this right. Russians are offering to give us 'official information on her dealings with Russia' even though we already have that information? Is that what is so scandalous, offering information already known?"

"So, Russians are offering official information already in the public domain on a public person who is running for president and that is somehow more significant than Russians providing personal information on a private citizen who is also running for president?"

Those are leading questions. As a lawyer, as a legislator, and as a parent, child, or co-worker, you have to deal with the facts as you have them. The facts were that email existed and had to be explored. It was best explored with former attorney general Sessions using leading questions that directed him in a certain way and with the answer and significance being embedded in the question. That is the nature of leading questions. Give the answer and highlight what is important while getting the witness to merely assent.

THE COMPLEXITY OF WHY

We were correct to name our daughter Abigail Anderson Gowdy after Judge G. Ross Anderson, Jr. She may wind up being every bit as good a lawyer as he was. And she certainly has his innate sense of siding with the less fortunate and those lacking power and influence.

We were having a conversation recently about the aftermath of natural disasters and the human response. In particular, we were discussing looting. Some believe it is acceptable to loot for the necessities of life like food and water; that it is almost an implied social contract of "I will take this for now because there is no cashier to pay and we will settle up later when the emergency has passed." Call it a Jean Valjean defense.

Others, like myself, are more likely to argue that the crime of stealing does not become a non-crime because of natural disaster, but the punishment should be mitigated based on the facts. In other words, stealing is stealing but we accept that why someone does something matters, and we will adjust culpability accordingly, but not change the scale of what is right or not.

The issue here—as almost all issues eventually do—devolves to a question of "why."

Why did you steal?

Why did you kill?

Why did you lie?

On the one hand "why" is the most important question in the world. "Why" can mitigate a killing from murder to self-defense. "Why" can mitigate a lie to a necessary evil to escape a worse consequence. "Why" is in many instances the question that matters most and the question that matters least; it just depends on the instance and the particular facts. If you killed someone because they were snoring too loud, that answers the "why" question but it does not mitigate the wrong at all, and in fact may actually aggravate it. If you killed someone because they were about to commit an act of violence against a child, that not only mitigates the crime to a non-crime, it makes us like you more. So, the question of "why" is factually important. It is also important from a standpoint of human nature.

We are simultaneously wired to want to be understood and to explain. We constantly think that if we can just get our side of the story out, it will make all the difference in the world. We are also curious by nature. If we hear a couple is separating, what do we ask? We ask, *Why? What happened? Who did what?*

That is true in life and we do not abandon life when we go into courtrooms, boardrooms, parent-teacher conferences, or Thanksgiving meals.

In murder cases, "why" almost never matters except in self-defense cases. There is no legally acceptable defense to murder aside from self-defense, necessity, justification, or accident. But you can rest assured that it is the first question the jury has in both their individual and collective minds. People want to know why things happen. People want to know why you do what you do. People want to know why you believe what you believe.

In the aftermath of the horrific mass killing in Las Vegas, Nevada, I was asked on television about a possible motive for the shooting. To be honest, I had to think whether to answer the question or not because I see motive in some instances differently from the way my colleagues see it. Motive is another word for "why." I spent next to no time thinking about the motive or the "why." After all, what possible explanation could be offered to explain systematically shooting innocent strangers at an outdoor concert? If I gave you all of human nature as a possible explanation, what explanation could you possibly construct that would then enable you to say "Okay, now I understand. Thank you for explaining that."

There is no explanation that is legally or socially acceptable. In some regards, we do a disservice to acts of depravity when we try to understand the "why" because there is no "why" that would ever adequately explain it. As a consequence, I spend less time thinking of the "why" and more time thinking about how to prevent the act, regardless of a "why." But I am admittedly in the minority. The vast majority of my fellow citizens do want an explanation, they do want to know a motive, and therefore they do want to know the "why." Even when there is no adequate answer.

When it comes to persuasion, "why" is a dangerous question fraught with all sorts of pitfalls, promise, and potential.

On the negative side, you lose control. You are inviting the person with whom you are talking to dominate the next portion of the interaction. Think about it, you ask a child why he or she underperformed on a test or quiz. What comes next? While it could be "Well, I did not prepare properly," that's rare. More likely to come is a story beginning with the discovery of fire or the continents separating and incorporating all the things that have happened to that child since birth and including all the pressure they feel to meet your expectations and how challenging life is for thirteen-year-olds and eventually you regret even asking the "why" question. You may lose control of the conversation, or maybe that child gives you such a lame explanation that he or she essentially gifts to you a dozen follow-up questions that help you prove your point. You don't know what will come up and the "why" is therefore a risky thing to ask. Except it's what we most want to know! So, it's a mixture of promise and pitfall and we cannot help ourselves and therefore we ask:

Why did you wreck your car?

Why didn't you clean your room?

Why didn't you help me with this presentation at work?

Why do we have to watch the Cowboys every Thanksgiving? (Be-

cause they are on every Thanksgiving, that's why!) But why are they on every Thanksgiving?

Or my favorite from a golf partner: *"Why did you hit that club?"* (Because I thought it was the right club, idiot. Why else would I have hit it?)

When it comes to asking "why," you must balance the pitfalls of losing control with the potential promise of a gold mine of follow-up questions. Asking "why" sometimes leads the person answering to make admissions that show bias, interest in the outcome of whatever it is you are discussing, or a lack of a factual basis.

If the answer to any "why" question is "because someone told me so," then you have your ready-made follow-up questions: asking "how" or "why" that other person knows what they claim to know. If the answer to "why" is because "that's what I have always believed," you have your ready-made follow-up questions impeaching those earlier beliefs and what may have informed or instructed them.

Which leads me to the single most powerful tool when it comes to your persuasive toolbox and knocking down the arguments being made against you: impeachment. Mishandled, impeachment is the fatal flaw that makes your attempts to persuade all the more difficult. But perfect the art of impeachment and you are well on your way to being a master persuader.

CHAPTER 9

NOT *THAT* KIND OF IMPEACHMENT

CREDIBILITY KILLERS

There is a constitutional process called impeachment wherein a president, vice president, or civil officer can be removed from office and barred from holding office in the future. It is tantamount to the political death penalty in that you are either removed from office or removed from office and forever barred from holding office in the future. Hate to disappoint you, but we are *not* talking about that kind of impeachment.

There is another form of impeachment that is also housed in the Constitution within the general notion of due process and more specifically the Sixth Amendment, and this is the kind of impeachment you will need to master to become an effective communicator and persuader.

Think of this kind of impeachment as discrediting. Think of this kind of impeachment as undercutting, subtracting, and in line with contradicting, not corroborating. Think of this kind of impeachment as anything that makes you less likely to believe the next thing that comes out of a person's mouth.

Let's try an exercise.

Close your eyes and just think for a moment. Think about what makes you more likely to believe someone. We discussed many of these traits earlier in the book—traits like access to facts, believability, likability, and authenticity. There are other traits too. Some may be unique to you. What do you find makes others more truthful?

When I was a brand-new prosecutor, the older prosecutors in the office would admonish me to shave every day. My father gave me an electric razor to take to the office with me so I could shave throughout the day. Why? That generation—for reasons I never fully grasp—believed facial hair and credibility did not go hand in hand. Perhaps it was the Nixon–Kennedy debate where I have heard others pontificate that because Nixon had a five-o'clock shadow he was deemed less likely to be believed. For my generation, that sounds laughable. But trust me, I've heard it countless times: Facial hair equals a lack of believability.

But there are surely quirks and nuances that lead you to believe or not believe someone is telling the truth. What makes you less likely to find a person credible or believable? What makes you more likely to believe the person with whom you are talking? Body language? Eye contact? Too much eye movement? Long pauses with the eyes moving up and to the side? Silence? Too much talking? Beginning a sentence with "I really should not confess this but, . . . to tell you the truth . . ."?

What you find incredible may not impact me the same way and vice versa. But it is still worth spending time reflecting on what generally makes you more or less likely to believe someone and then, conversely, what you do (or fail to do) that impacts how others perceive your believability.

Credibility killers abound. It can be lack of experience, expertise, or access to the facts (someone who did not attend a dinner party commenting on how great the dinner party was). It can be a lack of honesty, whether intentional or unintentional (saying that the dinner party took place on April 31, when there is indeed no April 31). It can be reputation; previous acts of dishonesty, fraud, deception, or any act or crime of moral turpitude (we are more likely to believe someone stole a silver fork from the dinner party if they were guilty of stealing one in the past). It can be bias, interest, and motive. Would you believe someone's recommendation if that someone is recommending you buy a set of knives from the knife company they own? You might believe them, but their burden of persuasion would be higher because you know they have a financial incentive to sell you their product. That doesn't mean the burden of persuasion is unscalable, but it may well mean the mountain is steeper to climb.

Imagine a mother testifying as a witness in her son's robbery trial. And you have to cross-examine the mother.*

You would hit the facts first, of course. Was the son with the mother at the time of the robbery, was she present at the time of the robbery, or was she providing an alibi for her son? Those questions all go to what we discussed above, which is an opportunity to observe or experience any fact that may be of consequence. What if she is just a general character witness testifying that her dear, sweet son would *never* commit a robbery? How would you impeach her? You would point out the relationship, for certain. But would you take it one step further and perhaps one step too far?

---

* Actually, you do not *have* to cross-examine every witness called by the other side. And the better you get at persuasion and communication, the better your sense of what to respond and react to and what to ignore. But for purposes of this example, let's assume you take the bait and cross-examine the defendant's mother.

The old story goes that the prosecutor said in typical leading-question form: "And isn't it true this defendant is your child, and isn't it true you love your child, and isn't it true you would lie for your son?" (Of course she would. If Mom won't lie for you, who will, right?) The mom testified: "Of course I would lie for my son, but I am just so happy in this case I don't have to."

Being a family member or a close relation falls in the category of bias, motive, relationship, or interest in the outcome. It does *not* mean you cannot or are not telling the truth. It does mean you will be examined on that issue and it may mean you have to be even more convincing to overcome that residual doubt because of the relation, interest, or motive.

That is the general framework from which we will examine impeachment. It is worth repeating: Impeachment is the single best way to undercut the argument of someone you are at odds with and it is one of the things you must be most mindful of as others are seeking to undercut or refute your own arguments. In practice, there are three general categories of impeachment: impeach the *facts,* impeach the *overarching principle or the conclusion,* or impeach the *person.*

IMPEACHING THE FACTS

Imagine a Social Security judge reversing the benefits hearing officer 90 percent of the time. You read that correctly: an administrative law judge (ALJ) assigned to hear Social Security cases, reversing the hearing officer 90 percent of the time. In layman's terms, out of one hundred appeals, the ALJ says the person hearing the case at the fact-finding level was wrong ninety times. Either you have an activist ALJ or a hearing officer who isn't very smart. But a 90 percent reversal rate is not what you should strive for as a foundation for a respected justice or administrative system.

As a result, we had a hearing in Congress and one of the witnesses was an ALJ with that 90 percent rate of reversing the initial hearing officer.

I have to confess that I did not prepare nearly as long for this hearing as I did many others. Actually, I did not prepare at all. I was on four committees at that time, which in my defense was more than any other member of Congress. And I was not planning on attending the hearing because of a scheduling conflict. But the chairman wanted me to attend. So, I went and listened.

What I heard helped me understand how a judge had a reversal rate that high. He said, "One hundred percent of the women who worked at call centers had been abused." He said, "Girls who were paddled as children wound up with sexual issues" because the paddling "arouses" something. I did not know enough to impeach him as a person, although it probably would not be that tough to come up with something. So, you impeach the facts.

Who told you 100 percent of the women who work at call centers have been abused?

What witness testified to that?

What learned treatise did you rely upon?

Who told you paddling young girls caused sexual issues later in life?

Who told you it "aroused" something in them?

Where does that evidence come from?

Was a study done?

The takeaway from the hearing with that witness was that he liked to make things up. He felt; therefore he ruled. He did not make an effective advocate for himself, and there is video evidence to prove it (so, you can see for yourself). He reversed

Social Security claim denials 90 percent of the time because he wanted the claimant to win. It had nothing to do with the evidence or what had been presented to him. He wanted a certain result; therefore he was going to achieve that result regardless of anything else. While you certainly can attack the person, that can and will get messy. So it's safer to attack the facts upon which he based his decisions, and those facts included his wild factual beliefs about call centers and spankings.

Impeaching the facts is what most criminal trials are all about. You cross-examine a witness's ability to see, hear, or experience what happened. You cross-examine the police officer on the steps he or she took to secure the crime scene, process the crime scene, and send the evidence for forensic evaluation. It is different from cross-examining the person. You are almost conceding that the person is a good or well-intentioned person, yet wrong nonetheless. When you impeach the person your objective is to leave the listener not believing the person. Conversely, when you impeach the facts, you want the jury to conclude the person is simply wrong, perhaps even unintentionally so. Remember: Proving someone is wrong about a fact is much easier than proving someone is a habitual liar. I used to remind myself in trial that every defendant I ever prosecuted, no matter how heinous or depraved the criminal act, uttered at least one truthful answer during his or her testimony. Sometimes it was simply answering the question: What is your name? Bad people can tell the truth and good people can lie.

When you are talking to family and friends it is hard to impeach the person. It is adversarial. It leads to hurt feelings. No one likes being accused of having a motive, having a bias, having an interest in the outcome, or being untruthful. There is really no easy way to make those accusations. So rather than focus on the speaker, you focus on the facts.

I have been blessed with three sisters: Laura, Caroline, and Elizabeth. All three are caring, wonderful people, and my mom will be very happy and proud that I wrote that!

We get along almost all of the time, largely because they follow politics but I don't, so I can plead ignorance when they ask me a question.

But sometimes you have to cross-examine people you love and impeach fact patterns even if they are being presented by your own family.

SISTER: Mom wants a Roku for her birthday.

ME: Mom doesn't know what a Roku is. She thinks it's the character from *Star Wars*. How do you know what Mom wants for her birthday?

SISTER: If you would call her more often, you would know she wants a Roku, so she can watch Netflix.

ME: How many times do I need to call Mom to know you don't need a Roku to watch Netflix?

SISTER: She thinks she does.

ME: After you convinced her she doesn't, what did she then say she wanted for her birthday?

SISTER: She wants a Roku for her birthday.

ME: You do realize you will still need the Netflix account, don't you?

SISTER: [Silence]

ME: Have you identified which shows she wants to watch? Hulu or Amazon Prime might be better, right?

SISTER: [Pause.] She wants a Roku.

ME: Well, how about I get her a Netflix subscription for her computer and give her one of my old Roku remotes that doesn't work anymore and then everyone is happy. How's that?

SISTER: [Dial tone.]

Impeaching the facts is tricky. The key is to keep the focus on the facts and not allow it to be ad hominem. Too often when things are going slowly on the facts because you can't make your point, we revert to the personal.

Asking "how do you know that" is usually safe, isn't it? It's a fair question. It's not personal.

Then you can examine or impeach how someone knows that. If it's hearsay or the information was gathered from someone else, that is your line of impeachment. How does the person who told you know it's true? If it's anecdotal, you have to be careful, but something happening once does not a trend make. Are there any studies on it? Research from reputable sources? "I heard it from a reliable source." Who? Just so I can have a sense of how "reliable" that source may be. Many opinions or beliefs are passed off as fact. It is hard to cross-examine or impeach someone's personal beliefs or opinions without it devolving into personal impeachment. The key is to keep your cross-examination as fact centric, rather than ad hominem, as possible and never cease to ask the source of and reliability of those facts.

How do you know that?

What are the limits of your knowledge?

That is how a philosopher would ask it. We aren't philosophers but we should strive to find our own way of asking those two vital questions.

IMPEACHING THE CONCLUSION

The second category of impeachment is to impeach the conclusion your opponent is trying to reach using those facts. It's as if you acknowledge the person is credible, the facts are reliable, but you still reach diametrically different conclusions and you seek to impeach the conclusions reached on the other side.

I served with Rep. Joaquin Castro in Congress generally and on the House Intelligence Committee in particular. We don't agree on much politically but he was affable, prepared, and an effective questioner during the Russia investigation for the Democrats. I do not know his brother, Julian, except to know he was the mayor of San Antonio, Texas, the secretary of HUD under President Obama, and a presidential candidate. He was also a witness at a House Judiciary Committee hearing on the issue of immigration. The issue was a path to citizenship, the Senate immigration bill, Deferred Action for Childhood Arrivals (DACA), and how our country would handle children brought to this country before the legal age of accountability. The talking point on the Democratic side was a "path to citizenship for fourteen million aspiring Americans." That was the theme on the Democratic side of the aisle; highlight the academic, military, and other accomplishments of Dreamers and use that to argue by extrapolation for citizenship for the entire undocumented population.

I did not know enough about the panel participants to impeach them personally; nor would it have been effective. And some of their facts were accurate. There have been Dreamer valedictorians. There have been Dreamers that sought to serve our country in the military. There are Dreamers who know no country other than this one, who speak no language other than English, and have nowhere to "go back to" if their status is in jeopardy here.

What I did disagree with was the conclusion they were seeking to reach: that because some of the fourteen million had achieved great accomplishments, that necessarily means all fourteen million should be on a path to citizenship. Only in DC politics can fourteen million of any group be homogenous and all pass a background check. Only in DC politics would you equate someone who was brought to this country as a one-year-old and lived here without incident with someone who crossed the border at age fifteen only six months ago and treat the two the same. The conclusion did not follow logically. The conclusion followed perfectly when it came to politics: Cast Republicans as heartless for insisting that all "fourteen million aspiring Americans" are not similarly situated.

You would not want to attack the witness; therefore you can rule out impeaching the person. It serves no purpose and is unnecessary to proving your point. You also are not impeaching the fact that, yes, many within the fourteen million undocumented population have and will achieve great things. Rather, you are impeaching the conclusion reached by Secretary Castro and others that because *some* have achieved, therefore *all* fourteen million should benefit. The witness is a fine person. I don't even necessarily quarrel with his facts. I disagree with and therefore will impeach the conclusion the witness is reaching and, therefore, asking you to reach.

Whenever you ask someone to provide the causal link or the connection between the facts they are relying on and what they are asking for, you are impeaching the conclusion rather than the person or the underlying facts.

IMPEACHING THE PERSON

I've saved the best, and hardest, for last, as impeaching the person is the most entertaining form of impeachment for spectators. It's personal. It's potentially ad hominem. It's as close to hand-to-hand combat as many will ever come. Done correctly, it is devastating to your opponent. Done incorrectly, it is devastating to what you are trying to accomplish.

Peter Strzok was a Special Agent with the Federal Bureau of

Investigation (FBI). Agent Strzok was assigned to two significant investigations in 2016: (1) the investigation into whether then secretary of state Hillary Clinton mishandled classified information and (2) whether Russia interfered with our 2016 general election and, if so, whether anyone connected with the campaign of Donald J. Trump conspired, colluded, or coordinated with any Russian state actors.

Agent Strzok testified publicly before a joint session of the House Judiciary Committee and the House Committee on Oversight and Government Reform. I was on both committees and the chairman of the latter. Put the public hearing you may have seen out of your mind for a moment. There was a private deposition taken of Agent Strzok before that public hearing and it is that private deposition I want to focus on.

I want to take you behind closed doors to that daylong deposition of Agent Strzok and the impeachment of him as a witness. Admittedly, there was a lot to work with when it came to impeaching Agent Strzok.

Agent Strzok wrote in a text that Secretary Clinton should win the general election 100,000,000 to 0 against then candidate Trump. What impeachment principle does that illustrate? Bias? Interest in the outcome?

Strzok wrote that he could smell Trump supporters in a Virginia Walmart.

Strzok promised Trump would not be elected president. He promised to stop it from happening.

Strzok discussed an "insurance policy" in the "unlikely" event that Trump won the general election.

Strzok wanted to work on the Russia investigation because it might lead to Trump's impeachment, but he was generally not interested in working on just another case where a foreign country tried to undermine the principles of participatory democracy.

And Strzok was dismissed from Special Counsel Robert Mueller's investigation as soon as Special Counsel Mueller learned of the aforementioned texts.

All of that is fodder for the impeachment of Peter Strzok as a person. Does it undercut the reliability of the underlying investigation? You tell me.

Was the impeachment of former LAPD detective Mark Fuhrman used to undercut and damage the credibility of the entire O. J. Simpson double murder case for the prosecution? If Mark Fuhrman uttered racial epithets, does it necessarily follow that O. J. Simpson did not murder two people? The two seem logically unconnected.

By that I mean Fuhrman could have uttered racial epithets *and* O. J. Simpson murdered Ron Goldman and Nicole Brown. But the defense went to great lengths to try to impeach Mark Fuhrman as a witness, so the jury would be less likely to believe other things he said or have doubts about other things he was involved in from an investigative standpoint.

It is theoretically possible that Strzok was biased against Trump, that Russia interfered with our 2016 election, and that someone on the Trump campaign worked in concert with them. The three are not mutually exclusive. But having someone with bias, interest in the outcome, and a motive counter to Trump's electoral success as the lead investigator can and frequently will cast doubt on other decisions made by that biased, interested, and negatively motivated investigator.

As the Supreme Court of the United States held in *U.S. v. Abel*:

> "Bias" is a term used in the "common law of evidence" to describe the relationship between a party and a witness which might lead the witness to slant, unconsciously or otherwise, his testimony in favor of or against a party.

Bias may be induced by a witness' like, dislike, or fear of a party, or by the witness' self-interest. Proof of bias is almost always relevant because the jury, as finder of fact and weigher of credibility, has historically been entitled to assess all evidence which might bear on the accuracy and truth of a witness' testimony. The "common law of evidence" allowed the showing of bias by extrinsic evidence, while requiring the cross-examiner to "take the answer of the witness" with respect to less favored forms of impeachment.*

Bias is pervasive and almost impossible to overcome. When the person with whom you are doing intellectual battle is biased, you should spend as much time as possible highlighting that bias as the facts reasonably allow.

That is the impeachment of a person. It makes those you are trying to persuade less likely to believe in the objectivity and neutrality of the person. It also has the residual effect of bleeding over into the larger investigation. Agent Strzok's defense was not that he lacked bias. His defense was that while he was biased, his bias did not actually hurt the person he was biased against or influence his investigation. In other words, he was ineffectively biased. That is not a good defense to be relying on when you are in the persuasion business.

Regrettably, I do not think Strzok's bias impacted how many people viewed his investigative work or his credibility as an agent. That is my reflection on the sad state of American politics. It is also a dangerous precedent to set in other facets of our culture. If the burden is now on the target of the bias to

---

* See generally McCormick on Evidence, supra, 40, at 89; Hale, "Bias as Affecting Credibility," *Hastings Journal* 1 (Fall 1949): 1. See also: http://cdn.loc.gov/service/ll/usrep/usrep469/usrep469045/usrep 469045.pdf.

prove how that bias negatively impacted his or her right to fairness, we are in a curious place as a society.

As we discussed earlier in the book, persuasion requires a jury that is open-minded, and regrettably that is rarely the case in our modern political environment. Nevertheless the "jury" outside of politics is oftentimes much more impartial and impeaching the person has such a pervasive and residual effect, it is typically the most effective form of impeachment.

With Peter Strzok, it was members of Congress sitting directly across from him asking him about statements and decisions that he made. It was members of Congress sitting directly across from him asking what he meant by "Trump would be destabilizing." It was members of Congress questioning Strzok directly on what he meant by Trump would be a "f★★★★★★ disaster."

That will not always be the case.

Sometimes the person who you are attempting to impeach will not even be in the same room and so your objective must be rooted in the question itself. Sometimes you will need a third person to impact the believability or credibility of your opponent. I call it *hitchhiking:* using someone else to get you where you want to go. It is not direct but it is equally effective and potentially more so, because the person you are seeking to impeach or whose credibility you are seeking to undercut is not present to offer any explanation.

So, pack your bags and thumbs up, folks.

CHAPTER 10

THE HITCHHIKER'S GUIDE

COMEY'S CONSENT

Former FBI director James Comey gave the press conference heard round the world on July 5, 2016. That was the press conference wherein he announced no reasonable prosecutor would pursue charges against Secretary Clinton for the mishandling of classified information, and then proceeded to lay out all the reasons a reasonable person might disagree with his conclusion. It was unprecedented. It made for fascinating theater but it did significant damage, in my judgment, to the justice system. Law enforcement agents don't announce charging decisions; prosecutors do. Law enforcement agents don't hold press conferences laying out the evidence against a person not indicted or facing charges. There have been Department of Justice Inspector General investigations and reports on the way Comey handled the Clinton investigation. Comey himself has written and spoken on the issue at length. You are free to form your own opinion on how he handled that investigation, the non-charging decision, and the subsequent reopening of the investigation in October 2016.

In the aftermath of that July 5, 2016, press conference, Comey was called to testify before the House Committee on Oversight and Government Reform. What would you have asked him? Who would you have perceived the jury to be? What would have been your objective? If you were a supporter of Secretary Clinton, would you have impeached Comey? If you were not a supporter of Secretary Clinton, how would you have used your five minutes on national television with the head of the FBI?

I do not pretend to know James Comey well. I have been around him a half dozen times, questioned him about a half dozen times, and watched him testify and speak in other settings. That does not make one an expert on another, but it is valuable information if you are going to be questioning someone in the future.

Comey is smart. He is savvy. He knows the power of not only what he is saying but also what he is not saying. He presents himself as being above the political fray (or used to, at least). He was a prosecutor in the Southern District of New York, worked at Main Justice, was in the private sector, and ultimately was nominated and approved to head the Federal Bureau of Investigation.

So, how do you factor all of that into your line of questioning for a seasoned former prosecutor and law enforcement official? Keep in mind that there are a couple of big factors. First, I would be questioning Comey on an investigation he knew more about than I did (in July 2016, at least). Second, this hearing would be televised nationally and therefore the broader public is the jury in this case.

Several of my former colleagues and I would huddle together and come up with a game plan for asking questions before most hearings: Jason Chaffetz, Jim Jordan, Mark Meadows, and I would make sure the right person was handling the right line of questioning for our backgrounds, personalities, and areas of focus.

So, the stage is set. Comey has just had that explosive press conference, he is coming to the House to testify, and you have five minutes to explore every point you want to explore. I decided to ask Comey about the one piece he said was lacking from the investigation on Clinton—the mens rea or scienter necessary to prosecute a case. Mens rea or scienter is the knowledge or intent typically necessary to transform an act into a criminal act.

I would have to hurry to get it all in in five minutes. And when you are asking about esoteric legal concepts, you are somewhat at the mercy of the person answering the question. There have been lengthy court opinions written on mens rea and scienter. Those legal concepts do not lend themselves to leading questions. The non-prosecuting public does not traffic in those words on a daily basis. The difference between general and specific intent is even difficult for judges and prosecutors to explain in five minutes. And as a general rule it is hard to both educate and advocate in the same exchange. By that I mean it takes time, energy, and the patience of the listener both to learn and to change course. Think about it for a minute. It's a tall task for me to both explain what hearsay evidence is and to also convince you that it should or should not be admissible. Learning something takes energy. Advocating among different alternatives takes energy too. So, it is my rule of thumb that it is difficult to both educate and advocate on a topic in the same exchange. It's better if you are able to separate those into two discrete tasks. I did not think I could successfully explain to the listening public in a mere five minutes both what criminal knowledge and intent were and why they were present. Nevertheless, a lack of intent or knowledge (those are two different things, incidentally) was what Comey said was missing in the case, and it needed to be explored.

So, that is what I prepared to do. I wrote and rewrote the questions. I tried to anticipate where he might go. He would defend the decision not to prosecute so, necessarily, he thought those elements were missing, but he would also have to concede that some of her actions were consistent with consciousness of guilt. The decision to delete emails could be evidence of that. The decision to outsource the destruction of certain devices could be evidence of that. The decision to not seek permission for her email arrangement and to keep that email arrangement secret could be evidence of that. Her false exculpatory statements could also be evidence of intent.

To pursue this line of questioning would be tough, but it needed to be done. It was the crux of his decision not to prosecute, according to him.

On the morning of the hearing I did what I always did before major hearings. Nothing. I sat in my office and played the hearing out in my mind. *If he says this, I will counter with this. If he opens this door, I will redirect him with this question.* But I still had this nagging feeling that I was taking a legal approach to what had become a decidedly nonlegal issue. I don't say that approvingly: Legal decisions should always be simply that, legal decisions. But this had morphed into something else. And those same principles I told you to apply before you engage in the art of persuasion, I needed to apply myself.

Who was the jury?

What was my objective?

What burden of proof did I need to meet in order to establish my objective?

And what facts were going to get me there in the five minutes I had been allotted?

Sometimes those precepts of jury, objective, and burden of proof are in a constant state of evolution. This is true in congressional hearings, the courtroom, and real life.

As I was sitting in the hearing room, with the hearing about to begin, the jury, at least in my mind, changed. It was no longer open-minded, objective listeners honestly struggling with the application of legal principles to the facts uncovered. The jury—as it has increasingly become in the modern political environment—consisted of two groups and only two groups: those for and those against.

Was anyone in America left undecided about whether Hillary Clinton should be prosecuted? My questions were good questions if the jury consisted of law professors who had been on sabbatical for a year at a nudist colony with no access to the Internet. But was there really anyone left in the country that cared about mens rea, scienter, knowledge, and specific intent?

If the jury had changed, had the objective also? What began as a desire to test and probe the intent and knowledge necessary to cross over from mistake/accident/simple negligence to careless/criminal had become a reluctant acknowledgment that Secretary Clinton's fans did not care about that and Secretary Clinton's foes likely did not either. And when I say *did not care,* both supporters and detractors cared about the *result,* but arguably not so much to go back through the analysis. That is the difficulty of moving from the process-centric justice system to the results-centric political system. In the justice system, the process is every bit as important as the result. It is, after all, the system where evidence is suppressed even though it is found, relevant, and material. The justice system is where confessions are excluded even though you earnestly believe you have the right person committing the crime—because process *matters* in the justice system. The majesty and uniqueness of our justice system is that *how* you do things matters every bit as much as the result you achieve. The end does not justify the means. Our justice system requires not only that you catch the right person for the right crime, but that you must also do it the right way. The old adage is that it is better for ninety-nine guilty people to go free than for one innocent person to be wrongfully accused and convicted.

But alas, this is not the justice system. This is politics, and the result is all that matters, whether you like it (or agree with it) or not. In politics, there is no book on right process and procedure. There is simply an election and it is incumbent on us as voters to employ and enforce our own rule book.

What Comey had said about *no reasonable prosecutor would prosecute this case* had essentially guaranteed that even a reasonable prosecutor who disagreed with him would never be able to successfully litigate that case. You cannot unring that bell "no reasonable prosecutor."

There would need to be a brand-new objective because there was a brand-new jury. At minimum, I would need to acknowledge that the jury I had hoped to be addressing did not exist.

While then chairman Jason Chaffetz was giving his opening remarks, I had to recalibrate my five minutes' worth of questions. What I had prepared would have been great in a room full of philosophers or perhaps even in front of a jury honestly struggling with the right thing to do. But that wasn't where I found myself. It took me way too long to come to that glaring reality, but at least I had a couple of minutes to pivot to pure impeachment of the person using someone else—or as I like to call it, *hitchhiking*. So, I scribbled furiously on a piece of paper. All of the preparation done ahead of time was worthless. This was going to be impeachment of one person by using another person—impeachment of Clinton using Comey.

I will abbreviate some of his responses but strive to capture the essence of what the jury heard. You should watch the exchange in its entirety to judge for yourself whether my summary is fair and accurate.

ME: When Secretary Clinton said she never sent or received any classified information over her private email. Was that true?

COMEY: No.

ME: Secretary Clinton said there was nothing marked classified on her emails. Was that true?

COMEY: No.

ME: Secretary Clinton said, "I did not email any classified material to anyone on my email. There is no classified material." Was that true?

COMEY: No.

ME: Secretary Clinton said she used just one device. Was that true?

COMEY: No.

ME: Secretary Clinton said all work-related emails were returned to the State Department. Was that true?

COMEY: No.

ME: Secretary Clinton said neither she nor anyone else deleted work-related emails from her personal email account. Was that true?

COMEY: No.

ME: Secretary Clinton said her lawyers read every one of the emails and were overly inclusive. Did her lawyers read the email content individually?

COMEY: No.

As you can see, using someone else—or rather, *something else*—to undercut the believability of someone you want to impeach denies the person whose credibility is being attacked the chance to defend or explain. In this case, I knew Jim Comey was not going to defend Secretary Clinton's failure to recall certain facts, and I knew he would have concluded that she could do that for herself some other time or he would conclude she could have gotten it right when asked about it the first time. But Comey was not going to offer any defenses for Clinton's answers. He was merely going to recite what they were.

Over time, the objective evolved from discussing requisite elements needed for a prosecution to discussing whether or not Hillary Clinton was truthful. The jury was twofold: (1) Republicans who needed something to pivot to since there would be no formal criminal proceeding, and (2) open-minded Americans who may have liked Secretary Clinton's policies but were unsure of her reliability. That is what is so destructive about impeachment (or at least should be)—that someone who has not told the truth in the past may not be likely to tell the truth in the future. In other words, it's great that you like her policies, but how certain are you that she really believes what she is saying given the instances of falsity in the past?

I never said she lied. I used her words and then asked the person who was responsible for the investigation whether she was truthful or not. Additionally, I positioned the answer to the question within the question itself. One example of a falsity would have been relevant but not dispositive. But layers and layers of falsity—especially on an issue so easily deflected with the truth—may indeed have an impact on all of those listening.

REPUTATION AND OPINIONS

Impeachment by hitchhiking is powerful. It is also not very common. Typically, in life, the person whose credibility is in question will be in the room, and will speak up and take over his or her own defense accordingly. When you use others to impeach, the object of your impeachment is powerless to correct, to explain, or to mitigate. The settings where hitchhiking can happen—namely courtrooms, congressional hearings, or conversations where someone whose credibility is at issue is not present—have unique sets of rules, which aren't found in family dens or office break rooms. But the concept survives and permeates.

It worked with Comey and Clinton and it also works on the other side of the aisle.

President Trump is fact-checked by the media on a daily basis. In fact, some media accounts keep a running total of what they believe to be falsehoods. The desired impact of that is much like it was with Secretary Clinton: to cast a wide net of doubt over what the person is saying.

This is why that paraphrase from Friedrich Nietzsche is always reverberating through my mind because it is so true about human nature. *It's not that I am upset you lied to me, it is that I am upset I don't know when I can believe you in the future.* That is the destructiveness of hitchhiking and impeaching in general.

The power and destructiveness of impeachment is even more prevalent in our normal lives. People may currently have low expectations for our politicians in Congress and lawyers in a courtroom, but we have high expectations for our family and friends. Untruthfulness can lead to a lack of trust that is omnipresent and therefore colors almost everything you hear from that potentially untrustworthy person.

Nietzsche's observation about human nature and what the inability to rely on the word of others does to us internally is powerful. Friendships, marriages, and business relationships have all crumbled because what began as tiny mistruths eventually cast doubt on the larger truths. *If you will lie about the little things, won't you also lie about the big ones?*

Lies are like the single hair needed to solve a murder or a molar discovered by archaeologists to build a face to fit. A single lie can ruin an entire reputation and impact an entire majority's opinion. Which is why it's important to get to know the two first cousins to the impeachment of others by way of hitchhiking: impeachment by *reputation* and impeachment by *opinion*. Reputation is what you know *others* think about someone. Opinion is what *you* think about someone. Opinions are not nearly as powerful as facts but they play an outsize role in real life (and an undersize role in the courtroom).

Have you noticed how people can have opinions about some movie star's character without having ever interacted with that person? Based on perhaps a solitary action, a single false statement, or a tabloid's biased article, an entire assumption is formed from afar. In a mere moment, a beloved celebrity can fall from grace based on mere *alleged* character. This is the heart of an entire reputation and a negative reputation spawns our own personal (albeit sometimes unwarranted) opinions.

Many of us have been asked our opinion of a singer, actor, or politician after a recent scandal or our impression of someone we barely know—but what about those we *do* know? That's when the stakes get a little higher. Most of us do have an honest opinion on the truthfulness or believability of people whom we know, and there may come a day when you find yourself being called upon to express that opinion if one of your allies is under impeachment attack. You may find yourself in the middle of a conversation about whether someone is truthful or had access to the facts or drew the right conclusion. You may even choose to bring others' opinions into that conversation because it helps you persuade or defend and deflect in your own effort to communicate.

True hitchhiking is where you use the witness to bolster or undercut the reputation of another with facts and *firsthand* experience. It is powerful, but it is rare. Nonetheless, you should be mindful of why it is powerful and the beauty of impeaching others while denying them the opportunity to defend themselves while simultaneously embedding your larger objective within the question itself.

In the case of Comey and Clinton, you were simply left with a series of "no" answers, which has the devastatingly cumulative effect on the reputation of the person being impeached.

That day my jury was the public at large and that jury heard this about Clinton's truthfulness:

"No."

"No."

"No."

"No."

"No."

"No."

"No."

A reputation created. Opinions formed. It has a strong effect.

One "no" is relevant when the question is "Do you believe what someone else told you?" A single "no" is eye catching. Imagine the power of a series of "no." Imagine the power of what seems like an endless stream of "no." Imagine the effectiveness of having the listener or observer answer to themselves "no" because they have been conditioned that that is what is coming. There is a reason our parents made us repeat the multiplication tables fifteen million times. There is a reason we know the words to our favorite songs. There is a reason we don't need notecards to say the Pledge of Allegiance. There is a reason we can't get the safety warnings from the flight attendants out of our minds. Repetition emphasizes that the information being repeated is worth our attention.

Which leads me to my next helpful device in your worthy pursuit to persuade: the power of repetition.

CHAPTER 11

REPETITION, REPETITION, REPETITION

THE RULE OF SEVEN

I do not remember a lot from my college days for various and sundry reasons. But I do remember the names of my fraternity pledge brothers in alphabetical order. Why? Because I had to repeat it countless times at the demand of the older fraternity brothers. If they had demanded I repeat what I had learned in history or psychology class, perhaps I would have done better on those tests. But I aced knowing my pledge brothers' names in order and with good speed.

We are wired to feel redundant when we repeat ourselves. We apologize for it. Sometimes we even preface a remark or a story with "Stop me if I have ever told you this before." But redundancy and repetition not only firmly imprint the information in the mind of the listener, they are also code for "This is important so I am going to say it over and over and over again."

In politics, the old saying goes that you have to touch a voter at least seven times before that person will agree to vote for you. In the courtroom, if a point is important it will be made by every witness capable of making the point. If the issue is the identity of the bank robber and there are five bank tellers, how many of the five would you have point out the robber in court? All five if you are smart.

It's true in all professions and across all institutions as well. In advertising, they too have the Rule of Seven and the term "effective frequency" is used to describe the number of times a buyer must be exposed to an advertisement before it elicits a response, be it buying the product or simply remembering the message.

And it works. Do any of the following ring a bell?

"Good to the last drop." (Maxwell House)

"Plop, plop, fizz, fizz, oh what a relief it is."
(Alka Seltzer)

"You're in good hands." (Allstate)

"Fifteen minutes could save you fifteen percent or
more on car insurance." (GEICO)

It's more than just good marketing copy. It's pure redundancy. Some of these commercials have been circulated for decades and it's not because they're saving money on marketing teams. It's because they know that someone hearing something again and again establishes familiarly, truth, and trust. And you better bet that my first-grade teacher wife has those kids recite their vocabulary words again and again and again.

As it relates to persuasion, repetition not only imprints that information in the mind of the listener, but it imprints that information as being important and therefore worth remembering and focusing on.

THE RULE OF NINE

Gary Vannatter was charged with killing his estranged wife, Freda Mae Vannatter. Freda Mae had moved out of the marital home, obtained a restraining order, was looking for employment, and was planning to divorce Gary. On October 1, 1999, she had a hair appointment and, later, a job interview. She never made it to either; her body was found in a car in a ditch in Spartanburg County with multiple stab wounds.

Gary Vannatter had an unusual story to tell about how that came to be. But since Freda Mae was dead and could not give her own version of her murder, we would need to deal with Gary's story and impeach him. For reasons that defy logic, Gary testified in his own defense.

Let's do an experiment. I will tell you what his version of the story was, and meanwhile you can consider how you would cross-examine or impeach his testimony.

According to Gary, he was driving a car on a road and Mrs. Vannatter was driving a separate car also on that road. They encountered each other and stopped on the roadside. Vannatter testified that his wife offered to perform a sexual act on him, he declined, and then she threatened him with a knife if he did not reconsider. Yes, you read that correctly. A husband declined a sexual overture from his wife and then the wife threatened him with a weapon until he reconsidered.

But don't stop here—his story keeps going.

Gary Vannatter said his wife got into his vehicle and offered to lift the restraining order if he would take her back to their former marital home so she could call the police and drop the restraining order. The next thing he knew, Freda Mae grabbed the steering wheel and was trying to turn the car in to the ditch. Gary *somehow* managed to stop the car, but when he did, according to his testimony at trial, Freda Mae pulled out a knife and threatened to kill him. The car then took off again with her foot on the accelerator, with him trying to fight her off and "the next thing I know, I stabbed her."

"Solicitor, your witness for cross-examination. Ladies and gentlemen of the jury, please give your attention to the prosecutor."

Now what?

Where would you go and why?

The jury is crystal clear: It's the twelve women and men sitting in the jury box next to you waiting to hear what comes out of your mouth next.

What is your objective? You cannot highlight her competing version of the facts because she is dead and has no competing version of the facts. There may well be a competing version of the facts but it will not come from her.

You have to persuade your jury—beyond a reasonable doubt—and you have to impeach him personally and on the facts, don't you?

He is claiming self-defense—that this was a fight that began between the two of them: She produced the knife, he fought her off, and she wound up dead. That's the essence of his version. It is good for your purposes that she wound up with an autopsy and a casket and he did not even wind up with a Band-Aid, but that is the conclusion. That is what you will argue to the jury during your closing argument, but this is cross-examination. What is your objective and what is the means by which you will accomplish that objective?

PROSECUTOR: Mr. Vannatter, where on her body did you stab your wife the first time?

DEFENDANT: I don't remember.

PROSECUTOR: Come on Mr. Vannatter, you can remember that

your wife flagged you down to offer you a sexual favor, despite the fact she had a restraining order against you, had left you, was divorcing you, and was on her way to a job interview, but you cannot remember where you stabbed her the first time? Think about it, Mr. Vannatter—where was it?

DEFENDANT: I think it was in her arm.

PROSECUTOR: And there was only one knife in the car and you had it, you had total control over it, and you didn't throw it out the window, you stabbed her in the arm with it, right?

DEFENDANT: (no answer)

PROSECUTOR: What did your wife say when you stabbed her the first time?

DEFENDANT: Nothing.

PROSECUTOR: You want this jury to believe you stabbed a woman in the arm with a knife and she said nothing about it. No reaction at all. Did she say anything, Mr. Vannatter, like "stop it," "why did you do that," "that hurt," "I can't believe you stabbed me"? Nothing?

DEFENDANT: No.

PROSECUTOR: What about the second stab, Mr. Vannatter? Where did you stab your wife the *second* time you stabbed her?

DEFENDANT: I don't really remember, it happened so fast.

PROSECUTOR: You seem to have very good recall that she propositioned you for sex. You can't remember where you stabbed her the second time?

DEFENDANT: No.

PROSECUTOR: Did she ask you to stop? Did she say anything when you stabbed her the second time?

DEFENDANT: No.

PROSECUTOR: What about the third time you stabbed her?

DEFENDANT: (no answer)

PROSECUTOR: You stabbed her twice in the heart, Mr. Vannatter. Surely she said something when you stabbed her in the heart with a knife? What did she say?

This is repetition. It seems tedious and redundant. The answer doesn't seem to change, but the answer isn't what we are focused on with repetition. We are focused on the question and we are slowly, painstakingly working our way through nine stab wounds, including two through the heart.

You are not ever going to get Gary Vannatter to admit he murdered his wife. That will not happen, nor do you need him to admit it. He isn't on the jury and his judgment of the facts is irrelevant. What you want is the jury to become uncomfortable with the slow walk through nine separate stab wounds, the implausibility that a victim of a knife attack would not say something.

What about the fourth time you stabbed her?

What about the fifth time you stabbed her?

What about the sixth time you stabbed her?

What about the seventh time you stabbed her?

What about the eighth time you stabbed her?

What about the ninth time you stabbed her?

In reality, you are setting up your summation, your closing argument, your crescendo when you last speak to the jury. This cannot be self-defense when one person winds up with an autopsy and the other doesn't even have a cut. Never mind the sheer, utter implausibility of someone even getting stabbed and not responding to the injury. What do we do when we do something as comparatively innocuous, like cutting ourselves with a piece of paper? We have all done that, haven't we? When we have just a minor paper cut, we jerk our hand back, bring it close to us, perhaps utter a non-church word, and vow to never do something like that again. We do not sit there reactionless and then do it eight more times.

Repetition imprints the most important fact in the listener's mind time and time again. Picking the right fact to imprint is part artistry. In the Vannatter case you could have seized on the fact she had left him. You could have focused on the fact she had secured a restraining order. You could have painted the picture that she was on her way to a job interview.

My second favorite option would be to emphasize the laughingly implausible notion that a wife would flag a husband down on the side of the road and demand to perform a sexual act on him—or the even more laughingly implausible notion that the husband would reject the overture. Several law enforcement officers asked me after the trial why I didn't use repetition with that. Good question. Two reasons, actually: (1) No one on the jury was likely to forget that part of his testimony regardless of whether I reminded them or not but, more important, (2) it was not inextricably tied to the charge in this case. Stabbing was. And I wanted him to go through each of the nine stab wounds in detail, because not only did I want the jury to hear the phrase "when you stabbed your wife" as much as they possibly could, I wanted him to hear those words as well. Because repetition is powerful and maybe, just maybe, he'd feel something in those words too.

KEEP MAKING YOUR POINT

Repetition is hardwired in our human consciousness. The more we hear something, the more likely we are to remember it. The more we hear something, the more important we judge that fact to be.

Working against us is that part of human nature that doesn't like to repeat itself. We don't tell the same person good morning six times in a morning. We may have the constant good wish of hoping their day starts off well, but we do not verbalize it repeatedly. It's uncomfortable. It's mechanical. It's creepy.

We also do not relentlessly continue making the same point. Most of us do not enjoy seeing others suffer, so once we have made our point clear, we pull the starters, we take a knee, we quit throwing passes, and we try to run the clock out without embarrassing the other side.

There are, however, a few rare souls who are wired to push harder even when they've already won.

When I played golf with President Trump, Mick Mulvaney, and Lindsey Graham, I saw one of those rare souls. I've played a lot of golf with Mick and Lindsey. If we are playing against each other we want to win for sure, but we mainly want to have a good time. Mick and I help each other with our swings— even if we are opponents. Lindsey is quick to readjust the match at the turn if it is too one-sided. President Trump would have made a good prosecutor, because he fully employs the art of relentless, merciless repetition.

President Trump and I were teammates playing against Mick and Lindsey. The president and I got up early in the match and our lead kept building and building. At the turn, we were up something like six holes. That's a lot to be up after only nine holes. We made the turn, got a quick snack, and were headed to the tenth tee for the back nine. The president leaned across the cart. I *thought* he was going to say "Hey, let's give them a couple more shots this next side." I *thought* he was going to say "We won the front, let's split up and start a new match." I thought wrong. What he said was "Let's see if we can keep them from winning any holes."

That is what repetition is in communication and persuasion.

It is identifying a mistake made by the other side and relentlessly making them own it.

TOO STUPID

Jonathan Gruber is a Harvard- and MIT-educated economist. He is reputed to be the brains behind the Massachusetts health-care plan and later what would become the Affordable Care Act or Obamacare. There are no dumb MIT professors, so when it came time to question him during a congressional committee hearing, there was no way I was going to ask him about health insurance, premium support, or economics. Instead, I was going to ask him about something we both knew equally well, which is what he said on tape, and then I was going to ask him the question that only he could answer, which is what he *meant* by it. Sometimes even super smart MIT professors say intemperate and impertinent things and Gruber did just that.

When speaking on the healthcare law—how it was passed and why it was necessary to be passed in that fashion—Gruber said, and I quote, "The American people are too stupid to understand the difference." And for those who were brought up to not say the word "stupid," well you should just skip to the next chapter because he used the word again when he referred to "the stupidity of the American voter."

Oof. If he had said it only once, that would be enough, but he said it twice so my door opened wide for what I was to do next. While the American public heard it from the horse's mouth twice, if your goal is to impeach him, you want that same jury to hear it again and again. And again.

So, if you were questioning Gruber, how many times would you include the word "stupid" in your question? A lot if you believe in the power of repetition.

You might ask:

What does "stupid" mean?

How can you be "too stupid"?

Are there degrees of "stupid" with some being within acceptable bounds but others being "too"?

Are all Americans "too stupid"?

How could you tell which Americans were "stupid," which ones were "too stupid"?

Which intelligence quotient test did you administer to determine which Americans were "too stupid"?

Can the Stanford-Binet test show "stupid"? Or is the Wechsler test better?

I did not fully employ the tool of repetition with Professor Gruber. I did ask him about it enough to make the point, but he said other things such as praising a legislative lack of transparency that would capture the attention of the listening audience and therefore warranted some time. But if there had been no artificial five-minute time limit as exists in congressional hearings, I might still be asking Professor Gruber what he meant by "too stupid."

Repetition works if you have a winning hand and in those cases when you have a misused or poorly thought word, you should run spades until you have no cards left.

CHAPTER 12

A WORD IS WORTH A THOUSAND WORDS

EAT YOUR WORDS

Not very many people have heard of the Chemical Safety and Hazard Investigation Board (CSB) and I would have been included in that lucky group of "not very many," but unfortunately the then chairman of the House Oversight and Government Reform Committee, Jason Chaffetz, had heard of that board and thought it would be a good idea to have a hearing on what the board had been up to—and it was not going to be pretty.

To my everlasting chagrin, he also thought it was important to have me attend that hearing. It was 2015, and I was minding my own business in my office in DC when Chairman Chaffetz called and said, "I need you to run down here real quick and question this witness."

"Well, why don't you do it, Jason?"

"Because you would be better at it," he said.

Kudos to Jason for knowing flattery will get you almost everywhere in life and for knowing a former placekicker for

Brigham Young University needed a prosecutor to help him on that particular day.

The issue was the use of personal email by the then chairman of the Chemical Safety and Hazard Investigation Board. All I had were a couple of sentences from him when he had been questioned in the past:

> In June of 2014 you were asked by Chairman Chaffetz, Have you ever used personal email for official business or communication?" And your answer was "Well, yes, out of ignorance."

You are taking my place on the dais in Congress. It should be a mixture of impeaching the person and impeaching the facts, and, as you should know by now, the best and safest way to accomplish that would be using questions and *not* accusations or declarative statements.

You might ask, "What was the source of your ignorance?" You may then launch into a series of questions about all the sources of information and material designed to lower the "ignorance" of employees by clearly spelling out what could and could not be done via personal email. You might ask whether he had consulted any handbooks or training manuals to better inform him on what he could and could not do.

He provided you with the word "ignorance."

It was his word, not yours. Make him own that word.

That's what I did. And when I asked him about the source of his ignorance, he responded, "Well, what I found when I got into the agency was that it was a normal custom . . ."

"Who told you that with specificity?" I asked.

He responded using a word I would not recommend under most circumstances: "*everybody*" as in, "My understanding was *everybody* used email."

Certain words are just too big to make for effective and

precise communication. "Everybody" is a big word. It assumes that you (1) know everybody and (2) know the email practices of everybody—an admittedly difficult thing to do. Another example is the word "always." Among the definitions and synonyms for "always" are "unfailingly," "every time," "at all times," and "without exception." The word "always" forces the person using it to have foreclosed every other option and it's impossible to do that. It requires you to identify, analyze, and eliminate every alternative, and that is a big, bright, red flag.

The witness then tried to minimize his use of personal email to conduct official business by saying he did it at the "beginning" of his tenure. Hey, that's not an "everybody" or an "always." It's a little bit more specific, great!

However, this leads you to have him define "beginning" because you know exactly how long he used personal email and eighteen months is not a very defensible definition of "beginning."

When confronted with the reality that he used personal email after the self-defined "beginning" of his tenure as chairman of the Chemical Safety and Hazard Investigation Board, the witness conceded he was mistaken by saying: "Probably yes."

Oh boy! "Probably" and "yes" don't always go together, do they? With doing nothing but asking questions with all the safety that provides, you can have this witness own his words, own the explanations of those words, and own the reality that his actions do not match his explanations. All by doing nothing but asking questions.

Now, we learned earlier about the power, potential, and pitfalls of the word "why." No question can cause you to lose control over a narrative quicker than the word "why." But the power of asking why is strongest when you couple it with your own sense of direction. In other words, "why" is most powerful when there is no good explanation. Because human nature will try to explain even where something is inexplicable. Human nature is wired to want to know why and to explain why. The why question is devastatingly powerful when you can couple that human desire to hear the explanation with the human desire to provide an explanation and there is no explanation other than a person's own error or misconduct.

To the chairman of the Chemical Safety Board it would go something like this:

"Why did you say you stopped the practice of using private email at the beginning of your tenure when in reality you continued it for eighteen months?"

"Why did you say 'everybody did it' when everybody did not do it?"

"Why did you testify you stopped the practice when you continued the practice for six more months even after that testimony?"

There are a few key lessons worth noting in this exchange:

1. When you use the other person's words in the form of questions, it's pretty doggone impenetrable.
2. Don't use big words like "everybody," "no one," "always," "never," or "every time" when you are a witness (or in general, for that matter).
3. Listen for those big words. They are helpful red flags!
4. Clarification of terms is a classic question to use in nearly any argument or persuasive conversation. ("What do you mean by 'beginning'?")
5. "Why" might be the weightiest and most powerful of words when used intentionally and carefully—especially when asking someone to explain the inexplicable.

In short, words matter. I do not expect you to read the dictionary like my father made me do, although there are worse uses of your time and it will facilitate a love for words and their precise meanings. I do, however, expect and encourage you to fall in love with the precision of words. Precision in the words you use is essential for effective communication. Some words are acceptable and modestly advance what you are trying to communicate, some words are perfect in capturing your point, and a lot of words cloud, clutter, and otherwise fail to advance the argument. When you are making your case, whether it is at the dinner table, in the break room at work, or when riding in the car debating with a spouse, be mindful of the words you choose and be vigilant in looking for openings based on the words others use.

BIG WORDS, SOFT WORDS

As we've learned, certain words are just too big to make for effective and precise communication.

When someone says "You *always* interrupt me when I am talking," you can choose to address the merits of the fact that you just interrupted someone for the umpteenth time (it's not nice to interrupt people, but it's also not nice to talk forever) or you can seize on the word "always." You will invariably run into someone in life, work, or leisure who is good enough to seize upon that word and deflect away from whatever objective you really had in mind.

Wouldn't it be better to simply say "You interrupted me when I was talking"? What do you gain by arguing in the hyperbolic? There is a role for hyperbole in communication generally and in persuasion specifically. But that hyperbole must be intentional, not careless. And it must be just that—intentionally hyperbolic—with all the humor and absurdity intended. What does the word "always" give you in that sentence? You really were not doing a historical survey of all conversations with that person throughout the duration of your relationship. What you were trying to communicate was "Stop interrupting me!" The word "always" adds nothing except an avenue from which you can be impeached.

What if the comment was "You *always* interrupt me when *we* are talking." "Always" is an easy word to seize on, but so too is the word "we." "We" doesn't talk (unless you are part of the royal family and are using the "royal we" and I sort of doubt you are). "You" talk or "they" talk. But "we" doesn't. The "we" was a noble attempt at being inclusive, but it exposes a layer of impeachment easily avoided and really does nothing to advance what you are trying to communicate.

If my wife were reading this (and that is a very big *if*) she would say "Stop nitpicking and let people talk in a way that is comfortable for them! People do not hyper-analyze words that way." She is right in her own world where her friends are actually nice people, and there is not a lot of debating going on. That's not the world I live in and presumably not the one you want to excel in. So, precision does matter.

What are some other words that leave the speaker open to impeachment? The word or prefix "no" sometimes does. As in "no one pays attention to me." "Nobody asks for my opinion." What is a better way to communicate your point? Why not ask: "Why aren't you paying attention to me?" or "Why haven't you asked my opinion?"

There are softer words and a far softer method to get your point across, and in using them you can limit your own exposure to being impeached. "Maybe" is a good word even if you are definitely sure. You lose nothing by hedging your bets and you allow yourself an escape route. "Probably" is a soft word. It communicates probabilities in your favor without the risk of saying "always" and owning every contingency. "Usually" is a soft word with a built-in safety net too. Softer words make room for escapes, parachutes, or pivots.

It is worth noting again that phrases like "in my opinion" or "I feel" leave the speaker open to potential impeachment. Opinions are great, but not in a duel involving facts. There is a reason for the saying "You are entitled to your own opinion, but not your own facts." In the hierarchy of persuasion, facts trump opinions and feelings. I prefer to use phrases like "Do you disagree" or "Have you considered" or "Is it possible."

The point is, specific words—big or soft—can be the very things that trip you up or lead you to victory. Always—and I do mean always!—keep a keen ear for when you use and when you hear them. I have seen good people tripped up by big words and I have seen solid cases undercut. Communication and persuasion are hard enough without making unforced errors by choosing a careless word when a more precise word exists, and you lose little to nothing by erring on the side of caution.

SUICIDE, SORT OF

It is impossible to effectively communicate if there is no common understanding of what is being said. When my Latin teachers spoke Latin, I had no idea what they were saying. I have the test scores to prove it. But even if you agree on the language, you still have to agree on the meaning of words. It is essential if you are really trying to understand and be understood. It is also extremely effective if you are trying to stop or slow down someone else's argument. I never cease to be amazed at the difficulty some people have explaining words we all think we know the definition of. We use words every day that have multiple meanings and sometimes very different meanings from what we intend.

The word "decimate" is a classic example. Most of us use that word to mean totally destroy and wipe out. The historical definition is to wipe out every tenth person (*decimat,* meaning "taken as a tenth"—see, I eventually nailed Latin!). There is a big difference between leaving 0 percent and leaving 90 percent to fight.

Understanding what is being said, with precision, and making the other person define the terms, is a powerful weapon in wars of persuasion.

Jonathan Binney broke into Allen and Judy Southern's home in rural Cherokee County. He did unspeakable things inside the home that only depraved people would do. From acts of sexual self-gratification to acts of defecation, Binney is quite possibly the most disturbed person I ever prosecuted—and that is saying a lot because I prosecuted some sick people.

Why did Jonathan Binney break into Allen and Judy Southern's home? Well, that is a story of depravity and evil unto itself. I will spare you the specific details but suffice it to say Binney committed a sexual battery on an infant. But Binney knew he would not want to go to prison as a child rapist—he wanted to go to prison as a murderer. So, he broke into the home of a couple he did not know. This couple had done nothing to him. They were strangers to him and he was a stranger to them. But Binney needed a victim for his plan to go to prison as a murderer to work.

So, while Judy Southern worked her job as a rural mail carrier, Binney invaded the home and put his wickedness on full display. When Judy Southern got home and walked through the door, Binney shot her. She died later at the hospital.

After shooting Judy Southern, Binney got on his motorized bicycle, attempted to dispose of the evidence of his crime, and put on several nicotine patches. Why did he put on nicotine patches? Well, to commit suicide of course, he claimed.

That was what later became his story for the jury. Why did

that matter? For two reasons: one obvious and one less so. The obvious reason was that Binney was eligible for the death penalty if he broke into the Southern home to lie in wait and kill either Judy or Allen Southern. He was eligible for the death penalty if he entered their home with the intent to commit a crime like robbery or sexual assault. But his theory of the case was that breaking into the Southern home—during daylight hours—to kill *himself* was not burglary and therefore this murder was not death penalty eligible.

The other reason defendants in criminal trials use the "suicide" defense is they mistakenly believe the jury will have some sympathy for defendants who were so wracked with guilt and remorse that they tried to mete out their own appropriate form of self-punishment by taking their own lives. The nonlogical line of thinking goes something like this: *The defendant wants to die, therefore let's really punish him by making him live.* Yeah, I don't much follow that line of reasoning either, but defendants do try it. It is easily dispatched, however.

So, where to start? You may want to start with the obvious that when it came time to kill Judy Southern, Jonathan Binney used a pretty reliable method of killing. He used a gun. When it came time to kill himself, well, Binney decided to employ a means of auto-eradication no one has ever heard of before: slapping on a handful of nicotine patches and waiting for his heart rate to accelerate so dramatically that it killed him. In case you are wondering . . . it did not work. It was about as half-hearted and cowardly a way to end his life as possible.

You may also be wondering why Binney never got around to killing himself with all the time he spent in the Southern home waiting on someone to get home. That's a good question. He had time for lots of acts of unspeakable depravity but never could find the time to put the handgun inside his mouth and pull the trigger.

It is rare for the definition of suicide to matter or have any legal significance. "Suicide" is one of those words we all think we know the meaning of. In this particular trial it did matter.

Irony aside, the fact that a defendant who wanted to kill himself would construct tortured legal analyses to avoid being put to death did cause me to reflect on those words we think we can define until we really have to.

Which brings me to a dinner on a balmy night in Charlotte, North Carolina.

If you've ever shared a meal with me, you know that my light dinner banter can turn complicated fast. I was at a restaurant with Senator Tim Scott and two other people as we waited for the meal to arrive. Actually, I'm not even sure the waiter had come to take our orders.

There was a lull and we had to talk about something. My idea? *Here's something light! Let's talk about suicide!*

What is suicide? Can *you* define it? You think you can, but try. In your own mind how would define that word if asked to do so?

It's the taking of your own life, right?

But by what means and accomplished within what time period?

The bar at the restaurant we were dining at in Charlotte may have been full of people committing "suicide" but doing so very slowly. Perhaps they had been told to stop drinking, but had not. Perhaps they had been told to alter their diet, but had not. Perhaps they had been told to exercise, but were not going to. Perhaps they had been prescribed medicine for high blood pressure, but were not taking it. Perhaps they let their gym membership lapse or failed to keep their latest dentist appointment.

The dictionary defines suicide as "the act or an instance of taking one's life voluntarily and intentionally." Does that capture all of your questions? Is it a single act as the dictionary definition implies or can it be a series of smaller acts? What does "voluntarily" mean? For that matter, what does "intentionally" mean?

If I am prescribed a medicine that will in all likelihood prolong my life and I do not take it, what is that called? What if I take some of it but not all of it because I do not have the money to take it as prescribed? Would you then analyze the other ways I spend money and judge the fact that I could have forgone cable television and my cellphone and thus had the money for the full dosage? Is suicide then a debate about life's priorities and how I assign them?

What if I just don't like the side effects, and I make the life-affirming decision that six months without hourly nausea is better than eighteen months with it? What is "one's life" for purposes of the definition above and who gets to decide that?

We sometimes think we know what words mean until we are forced to define them. "Love" is a hard word to define. When I was a kid I seem to remember the old phrase, "Love is never having to say 'I'm sorry.'" Yeah, right! Try that some time. Speaking of suicide, try going through life, marriage, relationships with those you care about and never saying "I'm sorry." Be sure to let me know how that turns out.

We use the word "right" a lot. We use the words "just" and "fair" and "equal" a lot. But what do they mean? And if you were forced to clarify their definition, could you do so in a way that avoided exposing you to any follow-up questions or cross-examination about what you left out?

What do you mean by *everybody*? What do you mean by *always*? What do you mean by *they*? What do you mean by *suicide*?

How we define terms matters. It matters for successful communication because both sides have to come to some consensus on what the terms mean. Asking for clarification of a word or phrase could be as benign as simply wanting to make sure we are speaking the same language—or it could be a defensive move.

CLARIFICATION OF GOOD

Now for a less morbid way of using clarification for your persuasion.

I've been playing golf with some of the same guys for thirty years now. Actually, that may not be true. Golf is a gentleman's game. You call infractions on yourself. In some sports, "do it as long as you can get away with it." "It isn't holding if the referee doesn't call it." "No blood, no foul." In golf, if your ball moves once it's been addressed and you are ready to hit the ball—even if you are in the woods with no one else around—it's a penalty. If your club brushes the sand in a bunker on your backswing, it's a penalty. Golf is a gentleman's game, so you compliment one another's good shots and you ignore one another's bad shots. You take your cap off at the end of the round on the eighteenth green, shake hands, and tell everyone how well they played. That's golf. So, what I play with my friends must be something else, because it is more like WWE wrestling. You need thick skin, poor hearing, a short memory, and a total lack of empathy for the failures of others. Most of my friends follow politics, but they are great about not talking about it or asking about DC much while we are playing. Most. Not all.

As we walked down the first fairway at a golf course in Spartanburg, one of my friends asked me: "Do you agree America is more respected worldwide now than under President Obama?"

I had not hit a particularly good drive, so I was not in the greatest of moods anyway, but I could have just won the lottery and my reaction would have likely been the same.

"The whole world?" I asked.

"You know what I mean," he said.

"Actually I don't! What do you mean by 'worldwide'? Have you checked with the people in Madagascar? Chad? Iceland? And what do you mean by 'respected'? How would I quantify respect? Is there some way to measure that?"

"Quit playing word games with me!" he lamented. "What I am saying is, don't you agree our foreign policy now is good?"

"What does 'good' mean? By what objective standard do you judge foreign policy? Half the country probably doesn't think it is 'good,' so can something be 'good' if it's fifty-fifty? Are you arguing there is some objective standard for 'good'— some objective, identifiable standard? Or is good whatever 50.1 percent of the people say it is? Are you familiar with the debate between H.L.A. Hart and Professor Lon Fuller? Who decides what is good? Right? Just?"

He didn't speak to me for the rest of the round, which *was* "good," by the way! Obviously, I did not want to talk about politics as evidenced by my questions back to him. But it also illustrates the potential power of making the person asking the questions assert some energy of their own.

There will be times when you genuinely need to know what someone means by a certain term. Some words are so inherently subjective, you simply must establish the parameters before you start: words like "just," "good," "beautiful," "power-ful."

Having terms defined for you is essential even if everyone is operating in good faith. But it is not simply words that must be defined and fleshed out. Sometimes people want to have discussions or arguments in the abstract when it is in your best interest that the highest degree of specificity be injected into the discussion.

There are openings in almost every question you get asked to turn that question into another question. Seize on a word. Make them define it. Make them own the content of what they just suggested. Make them prove any element of the premise they are now asking you about.

The precise use of words is an indispensable part of effective communication. Words have multiple meanings and that is even assuming we all agree on the definitions. We oftentimes will run into people who use words in a way in which we are not familiar or accustomed. So, it is imperative to get clarity on any seminal words upon which any conversation can change.

We must be careful not to be loose in our use of words or we will be the ones doing the defining, and when you are defining anything you run the risk of leaving something significant out.

I am, as you can probably tell by now and if you have made it this far, a huge fan of listening. Your next great question is likely to come from what the other person just said. So, listen! Carefully, critically, and with an open ear.

CHAPTER 13

GOOD THINGS COME IN SMALL REPACKAGING

SHINY PACKAGES

I am not sure what the statute of limitations is for stealing a parent's golf balls, but I am hoping it has passed. My father routinely received golf balls as a gift from his patients, but he would not play them because in his mind they were "too nice to play." That made (and makes) no sense to me. How can a golf ball be too nice to play? That is what it was created for. That's like saying a German chocolate cake is too nice to eat. It was created to be eaten!

Regardless, my dad would stash his Titleist golf balls in his home office and of course that office was off-limits to my three sisters and me. By "off-limits" I took it to mean we were forbidden to enter that office *while he was home*. But if he was not home (and I could not ask permission to enter his office), then permission could not really be denied because it was not truly sought. To be sure, he told us it was always off-limits, but there remained the chance he had changed his mind before leaving for work that morning and just forgot to tell us.

Sure, the fact that he locked the door to his home office was some circumstantial evidence that he did not want me in there, but a doctor has never hidden a key where a twelve-year-old lawyer in waiting could not find it. At first it was easy to find the key. It was immediately above the door, hanging on a piece of molding. (I mean, really? Who hides the key right above the lock?) But then my sisters dimed me out, and he hid it a little better. But not good enough! I found it in a Neil Diamond album cover near his stereo. Look, if he didn't want me to find it, he would have put it in one of his Perry Como or Andy Williams albums. But surely he knew I liked "Cracklin' Rosie" too, so hiding it there was basically just an invitation to come on in.

And in I went to Titleist heaven. All those boxes of Titleist looked so different on the outside—but it was the same ball on the inside. Each year there was some slight variation on the packaging, designed to be either more eye-catching or highlight some technological advance. But trust me, the ball was the same.

Repackaging matters. It makes something feel new and fresh. It makes something more aesthetically pleasing. It makes you feel like you are buying something completely new and different—something "too nice to be played."

It is also a devastating way to reframe your opponent's words and switch the burdens of persuasion.

Many of us do it reflexively and oftentimes defensively:

"Honey, dinner is ready!"

"Okay, I'll be right there."

"I guess you didn't realize I have been working on it for hours?"

"Umm . . . I said I'll be right there!"

"Well, if it's too much trouble to come now, I'll just put it in the refrigerator!"

It's instinctive, snarky, and persuasive. It's taking an "I'll be right there" and turning it into an "I'm not valuing what you've worked hard on all evening." Repackaging at its finest and most witnessed (and you better believe I hustled to the kitchen right then and there).

Repackaging can make old things new . . . and intentionally worse. It's especially effective when coupled with hyperbole, absurdity, and illogical extremes. It is the taking of some small part of what was said and reframing it in the most extreme way. It is taking isolated or anecdotal references and intentionally converting them to impossible and illogical extremes.

Earlier we mentioned the congressional hearing on immigration, a path to citizenship, and what to do with children brought to the United States before the age of legal accountability. The argument being made was that there were examples of DACA children who had achieved great things and therefore our country was bettered by their continued presence and ultimate citizenship.

"But surely you are not arguing all fourteen million were valedictorians?"

That is repackaging in an intentionally hyperbolic way. And of course the answer is "no." Then you transfer the focus from those who have accomplished to those who have not.

We also mentioned congressional hearings on the issues of gun control and mass killings.

"Are you arguing there is not a single law that could be passed to lower the risk of a future mass killing? Are you arguing it's a fate we just need to accept as Americans? Are you arguing that mass killings will be with us always and therefore we should just get used to them?"

Truth be told, repackaging is perhaps my favorite rhetorical tool. It forces you to listen to precisely what the other person is saying. It forces you to use your discernment to identify the weakest link in the chain of logic. It forces you to use the dark arts of absurdity, illogical extremes, and hyperbole and link one of those to the weakest link in the other side's rhetorical or logical chain.

Some common examples?

Sentences that begin with "Is what I hear you saying . . ." are usually sentences that end with a repackaged comment you made earlier. Sentences that begin with "*Surely* you are not arguing . . ." are usually sentences that end by slightly repackaging something you actually did say but perhaps did not mean.

This concept is pretty common in courtrooms and easy to spot. Domestic violence cases are sometimes very difficult to prosecute. This is true for many reasons, including reluctant victims, proof issues, or dual arrests where both the woman and man are arrested and therefore your star prosecution witness is also a defendant. Trust me—that last one is a challenging case; you can't win if your star witness doesn't testify. Societal and cultural assumptions and expectations are omnipresent. Sometimes the victim of a domestic violence attack will reunite with the perpetrator, and sometimes the cycle of violence repeats itself. Defense attorneys know better than to flat out say "It's your fault for going back to him." That is too obvious an attack for most defense attorneys but it is clearly a subliminal hint to the jury. So, don't let the defense get away with the subtle and the subliminal.

"Are you suggesting it was her fault she was victimized?"

"Is it her fault she was hit?"

"Are you saying she somehow brought this on herself?"

"Are you saying she is not entitled to access the home without being attacked?"

This defense tactic of implicitly blaming the victim for what happened to the victim also raises its ugly head in sexual assault cases.

I prosecuted a man for kidnapping and assaulting a Realtor. He had kidnapped her during the pretense of looking at a piece of property for sale or rent. This kidnapping and assault took place over the course of days, and of course as the narrative being told over those days is relayed, a defense attorney is constantly looking to find some evidence of the victim's consent or acquiescence. The defense attorney will search that chronology for some opening, some weakness where it can be implicitly argued that it was not *really* a crime. In this case, it was a stop at a gas station. The perpetrator went inside to pay, leaving the victim inside the car at the gas pump.

The defense pounced. "So, you had a chance to run away? You had a chance to scream for help? You had a chance to get the attention of someone else at the gas station, a clerk or another customer?"

As a prosecuting attorney, this is where you need to repackage what is being insinuated and hit back harder than you were hit.

"Are you saying the same fear that gripped her while she was being raped over the course of two days just vanished?"

"Are you saying the fear she had that she would be murdered—as he continually threatened to do—left her and she believed she could escape with no chance of being hurt more?"

"Are you suggesting *she* is to blame; that the person kidnapped, raped, and beaten bears some responsibility for being kidnapped, raped, and beaten? Is that what you are telling this jury?"

What people say and what people mean are oftentimes two distinctly different things. If you add to that truth what people tend to do (which is insinuate without flat out verbalizing), then you have, at a minimum, three things to constantly be looking out for: the words said, the intent behind them, and the insinuation that lies beneath. Then, all you have to do is listen and be ready to use structure and form as your friend.

THE DARK ARTS OF ABSURDITY AND HYPERBOLE

Our daughter, Abigail, is one of the great loves of my life. She is kind to everyone, not judgmental toward anyone, and rallies to the cause of the underdog. Oh yeah, and she loves to argue. By "argue" I mean in the classical sense of the word. She loves to debate. She loves to match wits and, while our politics are different at this stage of our respective lives, I do recall the twenty-two-year-old version of myself, who did not believe in the death penalty, only to eventually become a prosecutor who sought the death penalty seven times. People change, sometimes. Life has a way of doing that. But the key to change is authentic persuasion, motivated by either yourself or someone else.

I don't know what the future holds for her but I know the childhood and young adulthood she spent debating with her father will serve her well (especially when that was balanced by having such a kind and selfless mother). And I know that regardless of what her political beliefs are or ever will be, she has exactly the kind of compassionate, caring, and advocating soul that each of us would be honored to have on our side if we ever found ourselves in need of a friend.

The confirmation of Justice Brett Kavanaugh and the aftermath provided plenty of material for our nightly father-daughter debate sessions. It also shows how our beloved form of questions can make your point while deflecting contentious situations into more productive conversations.

A normal conversation during that time would have gone something like this:

ABIGAIL: I can't believe your friend Lindsey Graham supports Kavanaugh!

DAD: You mean the same Lindsey Graham who supported Justices Sonia Sotomayor and Elena Kagan? That Lindsey Graham? You can't believe he supported the nominee of a Republican president, as a Republican senator, but you could believe he supported two of President Obama's nominees?

ABIGAIL: That's not what I mean. I mean you were a prosecutor. Don't you believe the victim?

DAD: The word "victim" assumes a crime or wrong was committed. Let's don't make that assumption quite yet. Let's let the facts come. Let the witnesses testify. What is the tool we use to elucidate the truth?

ABIGAIL: I don't know, but I am sure you're going to tell me.

DAD: Think! It's confrontation of witnesses and the right to cross-examine, right?

ABIGAIL: She should not have to testify in front of all of those men in public. These are intensely personal issues.

DAD: Don't children have to testify in front of their abusers in a courtroom? Don't domestic violence victims have to testify in front of the twelve strangers about the most intimate details of their lives and relationships? Is this witness somehow different? Isn't the allegation here just as serious as the allegation in criminal matters?

ABIGAIL: I thought you said, "Don't use the word 'victim.'" [She got me here!] And this isn't a trial.

DAD: How can anyone believe any witness, regardless of the setting, before a witness has testified?

ABIGAIL: She had already testified by the time your friend Lindsey made his speech.

DAD: Yes, she had. Aren't you glad Lindsey at least waited until the witnesses spoke before he made any credibility assessments? Isn't that what fair people do? Wait until someone speaks before assessing believability? Weren't there senators on the other side making credibility determinations before she ever uttered a single word? Wasn't it one of the Democratic senators who said: "All women should be believed"? How can anyone determine credibility before a witness speaks?

ABIGAIL: So, you are saying she is lying?

DAD: What is a lie?

ABIGAIL: Everyone knows what a lie is.

DAD: Good. Then you won't have any trouble telling me what it is if everyone knows, will you?

ABIGAIL: It's someone who doesn't tell the truth.

DAD: People make honest mistakes, don't they? People remember the right event but the wrong name, don't they? Have you seen the research on eyewitness testimony? They aren't lying per se. They really believe it. But they are mistaken.

ABIGAIL: She wouldn't forget being assaulted by a Supreme Court nominee.

DAD: Perhaps not, but one would not forget being assaulted by a nominee to the DC Court of Appeals either, would they? One would not forget being assaulted by an employee of the White House Counsel's office, would they? Isn't the DC Court of Appeals the second-highest court in the land? One would not be fit for that court if he or she committed a sexual assault, would they?

ABIGAIL: It takes incredible courage to come forward and relay these painful memories and someone would not subject herself to the attacks and the scrutiny for no reason.

DAD: On that we agree. The key is to explore, test, and probe the "reason," and cross-examination and corroboration are the keys.

Nothing ad hominem about that exchange. No raised voices. No personal attacks. No hurt feelings.

In the real world, away from politics and crime, people repackage what we said and meant all the time. When we ask our children to simply clean up their rooms, or come in on time, or be considerate to a sibling, our children often repackage those comments into the far distant hyperbole.

"You're right, I don't ever do anything the way you want me to! I am a total failure. You probably wish you had never had me." Most parents have heard some variation of that theme from their children. That is repackaging in the absurd.

Don't take the bait! What they want is for you to retreat and begin listing all the wonderful things they do. Resist that temptation. It is hard. I know. Remember, I have children too. But resist it.

The way I handle it is to calmly note, "I have set aside all day tomorrow to discuss all of your wonderful qualities and the incredible things you have done. I am simply hoping I can add cleaning up your room on time to that list." The bait seems irresistible, but you must resist it nonetheless. Instead, your focus should be small—*please clean your room*—rather than a decades-long analysis of all the other things your child wants to discuss.

Always remember, you are not discussing broad, esoteric concepts. You are not discussing all fourteen million undocumented people living in the country. You are discussing either the one who aspires to join the military and serve a country he or she has no citizenship in, or the one who showed continued disregard for our country and our laws by hurting an innocent American. You are not discussing what the Second Amendment means. You are discussing the fourteen children who were just killed. You are not discussing the psychological and social benefits of having a clean room. You are discussing a clean room before their grandparents arrive. Remember, the more specific the comment, the easier it is to avoid others' efforts to repackage what you said.

That being said, repackaging can work wonders with the intentional use of hyperbole and absurdity and, when used effectively, can turn the person with whom you are talking into a witness for your own cause.

In death penalty cases, the defense team almost always hires an expert in psychology and/or psychiatry. This can be for the guilt phase, the sentencing phase, or both, but it is most commonly used in the sentencing phase when the defense is trying to convince the jury not to sentence the defendant to death.

Nearly every time, the psychiatrist finds some mental illness that, in the expert's judgment, either mitigates the crimes or at least hints to the jury that this person is really not responsible for what he or she did. There is a defense of insanity in criminal cases and that defense means the defendant is not able to distinguish right from wrong and therefore cannot be guilty of a crime. But if we are in the sentencing phase, that argument has already been tried and lost and they have moved to sheer mitigation.

In one of my capital trials, the forensic psychiatrist diagnosed the defendant with fetal alcohol syndrome. You don't want to attack the witness—in this case she was a very good, very personable and relatable doctor. You also don't want to minimize the condition because it is real and perhaps someone on the jury has a friend or family member who had a similar diagnosis. What you want to do is repackage the expert's conclusion into the hyperbolic and the absurd.

You take the facts the jury already knows and repackage the expert's testimony. (Warning: These facts are graphic but they were the facts in the case I prosecuted.)

So, what part of the fetal alcohol diagnosis makes you commit burglary?

What part of that diagnosis makes you masturbate in a stranger's house?

What part of that diagnosis causes you to defecate in a shower?

How many people diagnosed with fetal alcohol syndrome rape children?

Out of all the people diagnosed with fetal alcohol syndrome in the last five years, how many have shot total strangers because they wanted to go to prison as a murderer?

And then lie about it?

Repackaging is my favorite rhetorical skill. You have to listen and ease your way into it, but it can be devastating to the case of those with whom you are dueling.

THANKSGIVING CONVERSATIONS

Most families are politically diverse in one way or another. And try as we might to avoid discussing politics at Thanksgiving dinner, someone is going to decide to upset Mom anyway and lob a grenade.

"I don't see how anyone could possibly vote for Hillary Clinton for president."

"I don't see how anyone could possibly vote for Donald Trump for president."

How would you repackage that comment if you were trying to deflect, attack, or defend someone else or yourself?

What openings were given to you in that broad volley?

I have been present when both of those questions have been asked, and because the Cowboys come on every Thanksgiving

Day, I have a vested interest in getting those smaller questions out of the way so I can see something really important: like whether we win the opening toss and defer to the second half.

"Is your question, how someone could possibly vote for a person who was a United States senator, served our country as secretary of state and First Lady, and raised an impressive daughter? Is that your question?"

"Is your question, how a successful businessman, with a unique way of interacting with the American people, who fought through a tough primary field full of good politicians, and an even tougher media headwind, could raise hardworking, successful children and capture the electoral college? Is that your question?"

"Are you struggling to understand how a single, individual voter could vote for someone with that background or are you struggling to understand how specifically I could?"

"Have you asked any of the millions of people who did vote for that person why he or she did, or have you restricted your field of inquiry to just the myopic people you usually hang around with?"

There is a temptation people have to extrapolate. Because one police officer did not meet our expectations does not mean all the rest did not or do not. Because one politician violated public trust does not mean all of them do. Because I did not meet your expectations today does not mean either that your expectations were reasonable or that I will fail to meet them tomorrow. Be wary of making broad statements when you are discussing anything. It opens you up to repackaging and all the facts you did not consider.

Do not be too absurd or hyperbolic in your repackaging or you run the risk of being nutty and wholly unbelievable even in your fake outrage. Seize on a misplaced word by your verbal opponent. Seize on a fact that they are taking as true and that indeed has not be proven. And, last, do what I do, which is give yourself some soft outs and escapes.

I prefer to preface my repackaging with "Surely you are not suggesting . . . ," "Surely you are not arguing . . . ," "Surely it is not your position . . . ," or "Surely you have considered. . . ."

Repackaging is my favorite because it's both a powerful offensive and a powerful defensive weapon. It is best used by exposing the illogical extremes of what the other person is saying and it is even better when you can allow yourself the out of asking them, "Surely you are not suggesting . . ." even and especially when you know full well that is precisely what they are suggesting.

CHAPTER 14

WAIT, THE TABLES HAVE BEEN TURNED

STOP DIGGING

There are several old adages I have heard time and time again that are worth repeating (and some that are worth amending).

"It's uncanny how much luck good golfers have." (Talent makes things look so easy, we mistake it for luck.)

"Good facts make good lawyers." (You cannot win many arguments if you consistently have the wrong end of the facts.)

Some I have amended in case they help you fill a rhetorical need in your life. "A friend in need is a pest" (which I borrow from Vince Vaughn's character in *Wedding Crashers*), "A penny saved is just a penny," and "A house divided against itself is a duplex."

The adage I want you to focus on in this chapter is: "When you are in a hole, stop digging." When you find yourself in a persuasive pinch, start looking for a rope, a ladder, or a helping hand—and if that does not work, change the subject completely or start crying hysterically.

In life we invariably will be on the short end of an argument. We will have bad facts, or we defend something we do not really believe in, or maybe we don't feel especially persuasive that day. It happens to all of us. Professional golfers hit shanks and top tee shots. Actors flub lines. Gymnasts fall off the balance beam. Some days are just like that, and we need a plan for those days too. We need a plan for the days when fighting to a draw is a victory or simply living to fight another day is the best we can hope for.

As we round out the second part of this book, you should already have a good understanding of the tricks of the trade and some of my favored tools in the lofty art and act of persuasion. Now we're going to revisit them as defense tools—shields rather than swords, ways to survive (in at least one case quite literally) rather than ways to win.

AVERT AND DIVERT

Dr. Kevin Gilliland was a pledge brother in the fraternity we joined at Baylor University. We lived together in college, were in each other's weddings, and he remains the funniest person I have ever met in my life. He is the reason I took more psychology courses than any other discipline in college and he will be one of my pallbearers—but hopefully not anytime soon. He is also responsible for one of the most miserable experiences of my life.

Most of us remember where we were when significant events happened. And by significant, I mean events like Leon Lett trying to recover a blocked field goal on an icy, frozen field at Texas Stadium on Thanksgiving Day 1993. My wife and I were in Dallas to celebrate Thanksgiving with Kevin and Ann Gilliland and Ann's parents, Mr. and Mrs. Jim Bolton. We were inside a warm, beautiful house while it was freezing cold outside.

"Okay, let's go hunting," Kevin said with bags packed.

"Hunting? What? I'm a golfer, not a hunter, and I don't golf in freezing weather with ice and sleet pouring down."

Kevin assured me we would be fine. While he claims he never affirmatively stated there was a hunting lodge where we would be all toasty and warm, he certainly implied it. And by implied it, I mean he *literally* said there was an indoor hunting lodge with beds, electricity, and facilities.

So off we went in terrible weather with black ice abounding, headed for Jack County, Texas, to go hunting the night Leon Lett had broken my heart and ruined my holiday.

We kept driving farther and farther toward nowhere.

With us were Robert Bolton, Kevin's brother-in-law, and Ralph Ramsey, another fraternity brother.

Robert turned down what was supposed to be a dirt road but it was really a *frozen* dirt road and we kept going—and then he stopped. Sleet and freezing rain were pouring down on the car.

"Okay, we're here," Kevin said.

"Where is the hunting lodge?" I asked.

"It's in the trunk. We call them tents."

I would have killed Kevin then if I could have. I would have gladly served the remainder of my life in a Texas state prison because at least there I would not die of exposure and hypothermia. Probably.

We set up the tents on the "hunting" camp, which was apparently built on top of a nuclear waste dump because there was not an animal of any kind within a hundred miles. Not a deer. Not a hog. Not a bird. Nothing.

So, there we were in the tent as miserable as we have ever been in life, with sleet, ice, and freezing rain pouring down on us, with no heaters, and no feeling in any of our extremities, when Ralph decides it's a good time to tell us a story. Talk about a colossal lack of scene awareness or timing.

Because Gilliland and I are so much alike and have spent so much time around each other, we knew exactly what the other was thinking without a single word being exchanged.

RALPH: Y'all wanna hear a funny story?

KEVIN: No.

ME: Ralph, you're welcome to tell us a story—we're in a tent in the middle of bum blank Egypt with nowhere to go, so we can't stop you from telling us a story, but we will be the judges of how funny it is.

RALPH: This young man and young woman starting dating . . .

KEVIN: How old were they?

RALPH: . . . it doesn't matter how old they were . . .

ME: It does to us, Ralph! We want to know! Were they teenagers? Were the boy and girl the same age? Who was older?

RALPH: Really, guys, it's a funny story and it doesn't matter how old they were.

KEVIN: How long had they been going out?

RALPH: I don't know, guys, like a year.

ME: That's a long time, Ralph. Were they exclusively dating each other? If so, how long? Had they ever seen other people? Were promise rings exchanged?

RALPH: Guys, none of this stuff matters for my story.

KEVIN: You know, Ralph, the details may not matter to you. Maybe you have suppressed some of the details because of pain you experienced as a teen? But Gowdy and I want to know everything about this couple so we can fully participate in what you call a funny story.

RALPH: They were at a park with a swing set.

KEVIN: What kind of park?

ME: What kind of swing set?

RALPH: It doesn't matter, guys. Quit interrupting me!

KEVIN: It does matter to us. Was there a seesaw? How many

swings were there on that swing set? Was the park named for someone?

ME: Ralph, this is important to us. Where was the park? Kevin and I may have been there, in which case we don't need you to describe it for us. Or maybe we want to take our own families there and we are trying to see what all is available. Can we picnic? Is it public or private? What time does it open?

This went on for about an hour. Either Ralph knew what we were doing and didn't care or maybe he could not fathom two friends—about to freeze to death—interrupting what he had hoped to be a moment of levity in an otherwise miserable experience.

Regardless, Dr. Kevin Gilliland and I succeeded in preventing what was already the worst night of our lives from becoming the worst night in the recorded history of mankind by keeping Ralph from finishing his story.

Maybe we were a little obvious (and obnoxious), but there is a way to more subtly slow someone down by requiring attention to detail and facts. There is a rhythm everyone naturally has when they communicate or tell a story, and if you can alter that rhythm, you can alter the effectiveness of that communicator.

And while people do not like to be interrupted, they *really* do not like to be interrupted by someone offering declarative statements. Being interrupted with questions forces the speaker to evaluate: "Is this a legitimate request for more detail and more clarification or is this a delay tactic?" Gilliland and I were way too obvious that we were engaging in the latter. (I say were we way too obvious but it took an alarmingly long time for Ralph to figure out what we were doing.) You can get away with more subtlety but the result will be the same. Questions interrupt the rhythm and cadence of a speaker and being (somewhat) genuine in your questions allows you to slow the speaker to a screeching halt without him or her being any wiser.

DECONSTRUCTION

I like my brother-in-law Chad Abramson (well, as much as you can like any guy who marries your baby sister). He's a good husband, a good father, a good lawyer, and a rabid Clemson Tigers fan. Clemson has been on a roll lately, which makes life miserable around the holidays for me. So miserable, in fact, that I asked my mom if she would be willing to celebrate Thanksgiving four days in a row, one day with each of her children, so I could avoid having to talk Clemson football with him. She would not agree to do that. She said something ridiculous about "learning to get along with others" or "the importance of family" or "letting someone else have some joy in life" or something else that made no sense to me. So, I let it go in one ear and out the other.

If only Chad would stick with the facts, he would win most debates around our Clemson Tigers versus South Carolina Gamecocks conversations. But he won't. Because he can't. It is not enough that Clemson has won a couple of national championships. No. He wants to go further and state that Clemson wins the national championship while *also* playing the toughest schedule in the country. I could not help but immediately challenge him to a duel. I would let lesser issues like justice, democracy, or fairness go in the interest of family comity and tranquility. Yes, those minor, little things I could let go. But not Clemson playing the toughest schedule in the country. That's too much.

So, let's get out our iPhones, Chad, and deconstruct that statement in the cradle. Let's go game by game and pull up the power rankings of each of Clemson's opponents and then let's go to the Southeastern Conference (SEC) and see how playing Alabama, Auburn, LSU, Florida, or Georgia goes. Game by game, power ranking by power ranking. You want to make a bold assertion? Let's start at ground zero and back it up.

Think about all of the assumptions that take place in our normal, everyday communications. There is at least a tacit assumption the person we are speaking with is telling us the truth. There is at least a tacit assumption the person we are speaking with has some access to the information being communicated and there has been some vetting process along the way. What if you challenged those assumptions?

This is the heart of deconstruction. Deconstructing an argument is all about preventing your rhetorical opponent from laying any foundational blocks for what he or she seeks to build. One way to do that is to require proof before any block is laid down.

What if each one of those foundational blocks had to be proven by some quantum of evidence and then each evidentiary block similarly challenged one after another? What if we suspended the benefit of the doubt? Think about how hard it is to prove anything! We often allow others to make their own rhetorical progress until sometimes they are at the conclusion when we should have intervened sooner.

What if we took a "kill the argument in the cradle" approach and really forced each assertion to be buttressed? What if we were exacting in our expectations of the proper evidentiary groundwork being laid?

Ask, *how do you know that?* Not how do you *think, feel,* or *believe* that, but how do you *know* that? Requiring knowledge at every step of the argument-building process can wreak rhetorical havoc on those with whom you are communicating. So, it's a classic tactic to get you out of a pit of tacit assumptions. Remember how often we let people make questionable factual assertions as they are leading up to whatever the bigger point may be. Next time challenge the factual predicate (just maybe not at Thanksgiving when your brother-in-law is just trying to enjoy his holiday).

VICTIM MENTALITY

It's nice being the victim. Victims are afforded great deference in our culture (deservedly so) because most people are kind. They do not want to add to the suffering of others. They are not wired to keep pushing when a sensitive spot has been hit. Without sounding too crass and laying aside the victims of serious matters for whom we all feel sympathy and sadness, being a victim is an effective counter strategy on those days when things are not going well for us.

During the height of the debate over the Affordable Care Act, President Obama made a mistake, in my judgment. He attacked Paul Ryan and suggested Paul was less concerned with the well-being of children than he was. It's fine to have policy differences. It's not fine (but apparently acceptable in our political culture) to assume you love certain people more than others do. I think President Obama is better than that, and I know Paul Ryan is better than what was said about him.

Against that backdrop, the GOP conference was invited to the White House to talk with the president. All of us on the Republican side loaded up on big buses and went to the White House for a town hall of sorts. The president's comments about Paul came up and the president had an unusual response as I recall it:

"How do you think it makes me feel when you misrepresent my faith and my spiritual beliefs? How fair is it when you say I believe something, when I do not? How do you think I feel when you challenge my religion and what I believe?"

That was a good response on a number of levels. He deflected. He distracted. And he made himself a victim of unfairness. It does not mitigate doing wrong toward another, but I don't really think that he was trying to do that. I took it that he was pointing out that there was some intensely personal misinformation flowing both ways. I can respect that.

I have observed other politicians miss an opportunity to be the victim. It is hard to be both the victim and the attacker. Sometimes you have to choose. The best of all worlds is someone else is attacking on your behalf and you enjoy the lofty status of being a victim. When others perceive you as having been mistreated in some way, it has an effect on the jury. The jury almost does a recalibration in their own minds and they downplay your own missteps because someone has already punished you.

If you find yourself in a conversation and a misrepresentation has been made about you or a position of yours has been misrepresented, human nature is to sometimes forgive quickly and move on. Human nature is to avoid prolonged conflict. Resist that nature. Ask the person who got their facts wrong how they managed to do so. Relish the status of being the victim of misrepresentation. But remember: You can't be the victim and the attacker at the same time. Run out the victim card first and play it until it has lost effectiveness.

LEAN IN OR LAY OFF

There is another old adage that goes something like this: "Ain't no point in beatin' a dead horse—but then it can't hurt either." That may be true in theory. In reality, people do not like overkill. When you have won or are winning, don't throw passes downfield and run up the score. Again—and you will just need to trust me and my experience on this—when it comes to the art of persuasion, the jury and your fellow humans have an innate sense of when enough is enough. That innate sense of proportionality is also coupled with a sense of it being appropriate to strike hard blows but not foul blows.

I'll give you an example wherein a member of Congress did not follow that advice.

As mentioned, there were two examinations of former FBI agent Peter Strzok: One was behind closed doors in a deposition attended by only members of Congress and certain staffers and lasted for hours but outside the view of the public, and the other was the public hearing on national television before a joint session of two congressional committees, which was a train wreck.

It was a train wreck because it was always going to be a train wreck—too many members asking too many questions crammed into five-minute increments shortly after he had been asked about everything that could be asked behind closed doors.

We are all aware of the irony of a law enforcement agent talking about trust while he was having an affair with a coworker, just as we would be aware of the irony of a member of Congress criticizing Strzok for having an affair if he or she was engaged in the same conduct. Sometimes things do not need to be verbalized for the jury to know what is going on. You do not need to expressly tell the jury mothers would lie to protect their children. We already know that. You do not need to expressly, tell the jury that defendants have a real interest in not going to prison. Juries already know that. You do not need to tell the jury if you send a child's father to prison, his father will be in prison. Juries know that too. Everything does not need to be verbalized to be understood.

You probably also do not need to publicly confront a witness who was having an extramarital affair about all of the deception, deceit, double-talk, and concealment that typically accompany extramarital affairs. We get it! At some point you likely lied to your wife while this affair was ongoing. If you lied to your wife, would you likely lie to others? We can do the math and so can the jury. By harping on that one fact again and again, you run the risk of allowing the person the opportunity to plead victim undeservedly when you overreach and overkill.

There is a fine line between the form of justice most reasonable people embrace and the kind of vigilante retribution most people reject. Knowing where one stops and the other begins requires you to be in sync with your jury and know yourself well enough to tap the brakes. To be clear, I am not suggesting you feel sorry for the person on the verge of being destroyed, resurrected, and destroyed again. I am not encouraging you to back off because the person deserves some mercy or grace. I am encouraging you to back off because it hurts your own case to keep going.

If you have the facts, pound the facts; if you have the law, pound the law; if you don't have either, pound the table. When you divert from factual assertions or questions and steer away from good legal assertions or questions and fall into the trap of purely ad hominem attacks, you run the risk of the jury believing that is all you have—personal attacks.

Peter Strzok was not a sympathetic figure in the eyes of many. The only thing that could change that would be members of Congress asking poor questions in a poor way. Some members of Congress did manage to pull that off and this, ladies and gentleman, is overkill gone wrong.

There is an internal set of scales within each of us. When you feel the tables are turning not in your favor, use that innate common sense to lean in or lay off. We can feel those scales when we watch sports, and have a sense when the coach of the basketball team leading by thirty points with two minutes to go is still shooting three pointers. We feel those scales when one boxer has clearly beaten another and we throw the towel in the ring in our own minds even before his own corner man throws in the towel. We have an internal set of scales, which means most others do too. Don't turn villains into victims by ignoring this internal set of scales and don't surrender your victim status by striking foul blows of your own. The hardest thing in the world is to play by the rules when others are not, but the broader jury will reward you for it.

PLAN AND PREPARE FOR YOUR STRENGTHS AND WEAKNESSES

In every criminal case I ever prosecuted, there was some fact or assertion of fact that troubled me.

In every congressional hearing I participated in, there was something I really hoped did not come up. What do you least want to be asked yourself? What do you hope does not come up during the conversation you are preparing to have? What is that certain topic you do not want to discuss? Where is the weak link in your own rhetorical chain? Spend more time there.

I believe in having a plan and I doubly believe in having a plan for the worst-case scenario. What is your plan?

Most people are wired to focus on the strengths of their own cases. It feels good to do so. But persuasion isn't about feeling good—it's about a winning communication plan. What is the thing you fear the most and what is your plan for how to either survive it or pivot from it? The plan cannot simply be "Gosh, I hope no one finds out about the weaknesses in my argument." Be the first to know your own weaknesses and have a plan to plus them up, minimize the damage from them, or to pivot to more solid footing.

I routinely tell my friends and co-workers, "God does not

give everything to anyone." Rare is the person He made smart, funny, *and* cute. The best you can hope for is two out of three. Most of us have one out of three. Likewise, you will likely not have every weapon in the persuasion arsenal. But you should have one you feel most comfortable using. Nurture it. Expand it. Refine it.

Mine is asking unusual questions that divert and deflect. When things are not going well in a trial, a hearing, or just an everyday conversation, I will try to find some unusual question to ask that forces the other person to do some quick thinking while it allows me to gather my wits. The question has to be relevant, but not too relevant. The question has to seem reasonable, but just slightly outside of the center of the target. The question should be good but distracting.

For example, as it relates to the sometimes contentious issue of immigration, I enjoy asking others which crimes should be disqualifiers for either avoiding removal or remaining on a path toward legal status. It forces the person arguing against removal or arguing for a wide, generous path to status or citizenship to quickly go through the whole criminal code. Invariably they will leave some significant crime out, which you can then ask about. I try to do that with other issues as well: Find a question that forces the other person to do the quick thinking.

If you ever find yourself talking to a group and things are not going well, there are two tricks I employ. They are both extreme. The first is *silence*. Silence is the greatest attention grabber in the world. We have our own internal clock where we begin to get apprehensive if the speaker doesn't say anything. Has she lost her notes? Has he blanked out? Is there some medical problem? Why aren't they talking? I give lots of speeches at this stage of life and in almost every single one, I create a series of uncomfortable pauses designed to force everyone in the room to stop what they are doing and watch the potentially impending train wreck. And then I start right back up as if nothing happened. Silence is the single greatest attention grabber you will ever have access to. Learn the timing of silence—longer than a breath but not long enough that others think it's a nap.

The second extreme is the filibuster. We are taught not to interrupt. We are taught to listen. We are loath to jump in mid-sentence while someone else is talking. Take advantage of those teachings when you find yourself on the short end of a debate. The most difficult witnesses to examine in Congress and in courtrooms are those witnesses who . . . simply . . . will . . . not . . . stop talking. Juries do not like rude people who interrupt and they certainly do not like to be interrupted.

Just as you should identify your best communications gift, you should also identify your favorite persuasion tool. Which of the tools we have discussed would you enjoy most being highly skilled at? Which one could you see yourself mastering?

You will have bad days when you engage in the art of persuasion. The key is to minimize the number of bad days with preparation and anticipation. And when the bad day comes, shorten the duration by deflecting, holding the ball until overtime, or diverting the conversation with either silence or a filibuster.

At the end of the day, if you can arrive to the argument an active listener and engaged speaker and know who it is you are talking to and what you want to convince them of, my bet is you're going to do just fine.

PART 3

GO FORTH AND CONQUER

CHAPTER 15

NOT-SO-GREAT EXPECTATIONS

COMMONALITY, NOT CONSENSUS

I spent most of my life in South Carolina before going to college in Texas. Those are two very different states but the similarities in terms of what people believed religiously, politically, and fundamentally probably outweigh any differences. Sure, there were some things to get adjusted to: George Strait rather than Elvis Presley. Line dancing rather than the shag. Wranglers rather than Levi's. But the similarities outpaced the differences on the big stuff.

I did travel overseas some as a youth, to Africa, Israel, and Europe, but in some instances those were very different cultures as opposed to different people co-existing within the same general culture and political structure.

It was being in Washington as a congressman that opened my eyes in ways they had not been opened before. The most liberal person I knew in South Carolina would be a moderate in Washington. There was racial and religious diversity in South Carolina but nothing like there was in Washington. What I experienced in DC was people who had very deeply held beliefs that ran counter to my own deeply held beliefs. So, there was a choice to be made early on: Avoid those differences and try to persuade toward total consensus or accept those differences and appreciate them.

If I had arrived with my proverbial persuasive guns blazing—expecting to reach full consensus with everyone I met and evangelizing my particular beliefs per my South Carolina experiences—I would have no doubt left a massive failure. To aim for absolute consensus is not only a silly expectation, it's a disrespectful one. Washington showed me that while consensus is a not-so-great expectation, commonality is an admirable and reasonable one.

When I announced that I would leave politics and return to South Carolina, it was timed to coincide with my leaving town. I did not want to run into reporters or have protracted conversations with my colleagues. The people closest to me knew what I was going to do and that was good enough for me. So, I made the announcement and headed to the airport to come home at the end of the week.

I looked down at my phone and began to see text messages popping up. The first was from now senator Kyrsten Sinema. The second was from Representative Tulsi Gabbard. There were others and many of them were from my friends and colleagues on the Republican side. But the first and second texts I received were from two colleagues you might not necessarily even think I would know.

At first blush, you would wonder what a Republican from South Carolina would have in common with a Democrat from Arizona and a Democrat from Hawaii. Turns out we have a lot in common, just not necessarily as it relates to politics. Yes, we vote differently. We should. Our districts and those we are privileged to represent think and believe and vote differently. But life is about more than just politics. It's about virtue, and family, and the celebration of things we have in common.

Sometimes we fall into the trap of thinking persuasion is the final act of getting someone to fully change his or her mind. That is a very tough thing to accomplish. Having someone switch his or her opinion on when life begins, or the limits on the Second Amendment, or whether we should keep or scrap the electoral college is hard and does not often occur. What if persuasion is more subtle than that?

What if you persuade a person who once believed life began at viability to believe life began earlier? What if you convinced someone who believed the Second Amendment has no limitations to believe that, yes, there have been restrictions on who can possess certain weapons, where you can possess those weapons, and the nature of those weapons?

Don't get greedy. Have fair and realistic expectations in how much you expect to accomplish. Don't assume that what you believe is so powerful as to totally upend someone's own personal beliefs and experiences. Sometimes the greatest act of persuasion you will ever accomplish is to persuade someone that it's time to stop fighting all the time. Sometimes the most persuasive thing you could ever do is tell someone with whom you disagree that you are making an effort to better understand where they are coming from.

Remember, persuasion is movement. Seek common ground over complete consensus. It's far more achievable and in most ways far more admirable. Thinking it's going to be a wholesale change is a sure-fire way for your lofty goal to end in lamentable failure.

WINNING VS. SUCCEEDING

There is no disappointment in life quite like mismatched expectations. If I think I am getting a new bicycle for Christmas, and I get a nice watch, there is bound to be disappointment. That is no reflection on either the bicycle or the watch. Nor does it mean my parents didn't really love me. It means there was a disconnect between the two sets of expectations and that disconnect led to some type of failure, be it temporary or longer-lasting.

Most of my failures have been the result of unmatched expectations or of getting too greedy in my persuasion—of wanting more out of an exchange than what is necessarily owed to me or reasonably achievable in that conversation. When there is no symmetry between the expectations of the person attempting to communicate and those receiving the communication, there is going to be a painful disconnect.

From a political perspective, the rise of populism within both parties is, in my judgment, a symptom of unmatched expectations. I am most familiar with the Republican side of the equation, so those of you from other political perspectives can judge whether it is true on your team.

When I arrived in Washington in 2011, Republicans had the House but not the Senate or the White House. So that was the message: "We can't do the things you want us to do because we do not control the Senate or the White House. We cannot lower the deficit, and ultimately the debt. We cannot transform Medicare or Social Security. We cannot reduce the size and scope of government. We cannot provide a market-based series of healthcare reforms unless and until we have more."

Republicans wanted to start with the Senate. That's what we needed! We needed the Senate so a Republican-led House could pass bills and send them to a Republican-led Senate and those bills would be passed and then sent to President Obama for his signature. He would veto the bills and that would provide the contrast in ideology politics is so dependent on. That was the plan. That was the objective. That was what Republicans communicated. And in 2012, the American people rewarded that request by giving Republicans control over the Senate.

But nothing changed.

So, Republicans had a choice: We could level with the American people, have a very frank conversation within the Republican Party itself, or we could find a new something we "needed." We opted for the latter.

The new effort to communicate and persuade was that what we really, really needed was not just the Senate but the Senate *and* the White House. That would change everything.

And in 2016 the American people gave Republicans the House, the Senate, and the White House.

This was the chance to do all of what had been promised! This was the chance to meet all the expectations effectively communicated! This was the chance to do all the things Republicans for years had talked about doing! And . . . it did not happen.

Someone else can write the book about why Republicans failed to govern effectively. Someone else can write the book about the battles within the Republican Party, the lack of an agenda, the lack of a cohesive strategy. I was there. I most assuredly have an opinion but this is neither the time nor the place for that discussion.

My point is that the messaging, the communication, and the persuasion were effective if the goal was simply to win. The Republicans had the House, the Senate, and the White House. They had won. That is what they wanted and that is what they got. It wasn't the messaging they got wrong. It was the total lack of synchronicity with what was being communicated and what was being delivered. That is mismatched communication. That is failure.

Failure occurs when you get something wrong, be it the jury, the burden of proof, the facts, or the expectations. And at various times in life, I have gotten all of them wrong, but it seems it never stings as much as when the failure was caused by unmet expectations and a failure to recognize who the jury really was or should have been.

BREAKING DOWN BENGHAZI

There is value in learning from others' mistakes. I preach that to my own children all the time. You do not need to learn for yourselves those things I learned the hard way for both of us. If I tell you the stove is hot and it's still bright red, why touch it? If I tell you now is not the right time to ask Mom for something, because she is in the middle of her Hallmark Christmas Movie marathon, trust me on that. I learned lessons about communication, persuasion, and movement at various stages while I was in Congress, but I learned the hardest lessons during the investigation into what happened in Benghazi, Libya, in 2012.

Let me say again, because it is important to reiterate, this is not a book about politics. I did not and do not want to write a book about politics. This is a book about effective communication and how to persuade or move others. So, I do not write this section to revisit the Select Committee on Benghazi or Secretary Hillary Clinton except to point out my own failures and the lessons learned as a result. And maybe, just maybe, you can learn from my mistakes and avoid them yourself as you have your own trials, tribulations, and opportunities.

The lessons I lay out in this book—knowing your jury, projecting sincerity, having command of your facts, understanding the calibration between what you are trying to prove and what the jury or the public will expect, and, most important, having a clear, concise objective in mind before you start—those are all things I should have spent more time focused on when Speaker John Boehner called and said he was proposing a select committee to write the final chapter on what happened to four brave Americans who lost their lives in service to our country.

It is nearly impossible to conduct a serious, fact-centric investigation in a hyper-political environment. That is certain to offend Democrats who want President Trump investigated for all of the things they want him investigated for. That is also certain to offend Republicans who investigated matters related to the Department of Justice, the Foreign Intelligence Surveillance Act (FISA), or the Internal Revenue Service (IRS) and its handling of conservative groups. But I was part of all those investigations in some way or another and my position remains unchanged: *It is nearly impossible to conduct serious, fact-centric investigations in the current political environment.*

The first obstacle is that the jury, at least as it relates to highly contentious political issues, is not really persuadable and effective persuasion requires someone to at least have something of an open mind. Another indispensable aspect of effective communication is knowing, with precision and clarity, precisely who your jury is. As it related to the Select Committee on Benghazi, the jury began to get smaller and smaller as the investigation wore on. Republican activists were not happy because I never had any patience or interest in unfounded conspiracy theories nor would I accept meetings with groups espousing those theories. There are still Republican lawyers who are upset with me because I would not meet with their clients. That's okay—sometimes who your critics are is just as important as who your supporters are.

Democrats were not happy because there was yet another investigation, period. It is true that there had been an Accountability Review Board. It is true that other committees of Congress had looked at various aspects of what happened in Benghazi. The House Intelligence Committee, chaired by a Republican, issued a report. The House Armed Services Committee, chaired by a Republican, issued a report. The House Committee on Oversight and Government Reform, chaired by a Republican, had also issued a report. So, Democrats and the media could have done one of two things: (1) complain about yet another investigation or (2) ask why the previous investigations had left so many questions unanswered. The Democrats and the media opted for the former.

I believed then, as I do now, that there were legitimate questions worthy of answering.

Why wasn't a single U.S. military asset moving toward Benghazi, Libya, from the time of the initial attack on our ambassador and other diplomatic personnel until the time the Annex was attacked and Ty Woods and Glen Doherty were killed? This is a legitimate question no matter what your politics may be. Yet it was not answered by any of the previous committees' investigations.

Who ultimately rescued our personnel from the Annex after the mortar attack that killed Ty Woods and Glen Doherty? This is also a legitimate question. It was singularly important to many of the men who were rescued—that the right group receive the credit and the wrong group not get the credit. Yet, the previous committees did not identify the group responsible for saving even more American lives.

We all knew the attack was not the spontaneous reaction to an anti-Islam movie that had been released earlier and had caused a few protests elsewhere in the Middle East. That had been firmly established. What we did not know was how that talking point became part of the administration's narrative. The consequences were significant. Was it deliberate? Was it impacted by the coming 2012 presidential election? Or was it simple negligence when an analyst included the wrong headline, from the wrong date, in an intelligence report and it was relied upon? The question deserved to be answered and yet the previous committees did not do so.

If you were trying to ascertain what happened during any incident, you would want to talk to the eyewitnesses, right? Would you want to talk to all the eyewitnesses? Is there some limit to how many eyewitnesses you would want to talk to?

Recently, a Democratic former colleague stated, in connection with the Ukrainian investigation, that of course he was not going to have public hearings where one witness could listen to another witness and tailor and fashion their testimonies accordingly. Makes sense, doesn't it? You don't interview witnesses in groups, and to the extent that you can, you do not allow witnesses to know what other witnesses have said. It's called sequestration in a courtroom setting and it's routinely invoked for just that reason: to keep witnesses from squaring up their stories by listening in on one another.

So, if interviewing witnesses one by one is good enough for the Ukrainian investigation and good enough for courtrooms across the country, wouldn't it also be good enough for an investigation into the murder of a U.S. ambassador and three other brave public servants?

Why were all eyewitnesses not interviewed by the previous committees that looked into what happened in Benghazi? And why were some of the eyewitnesses interviewed by previous committees in groups and not individually? If it's good for one side, it should be good enough for the other, right?

Was more security requested for Tripoli or Benghazi in the weeks and months leading to the attacks? What was the State

Department aware of and to whom were the requests made? Those were fundamentally important questions to what ultimately became the only "jury" I cared about: the survivors of the attacks and the family members of those killed. To answer that question required access to documents. Those documents were in the custody and control of the State Department and could have potentially included emails to or from the secretary of state herself.

That is the real reason Democrats and the media paid attention to the last investigation into what happened in Benghazi: because the secretary of state was a candidate for the Democratic nomination. I do understand that fellow candidate Senator Bernie Sanders said he did not care about her "damn emails." I also understand there were people who were interested and were not on any debate stages and not running for anything, but with a vested interest in knowing whether more security was requested, by whom, and to whom. And to the extent that any of that information could have been in State Department documents and emails, those family members and survivors did care about her "damn emails."

The Benghazi investigation became hopelessly interlocked with the story of Secretary Clinton's email arrangement. That eventually led to the server and a thousand other stories thereafter. Asking for emails from the secretary of state about security requests in the aftermath of an ambassador being killed was an eminently reasonable thing to do. How else would you evaluate what was known and when other than by looking at documents?

Believe it or not, House Republicans on the Select Committee on Benghazi did not create the email story. That was done by the reporting of a *New York Times* reporter named Michael Schmidt. Schmidt also broke the FIFA soccer scandal story and a host of subsequent stories about the FBI and Department of Justice. If being a good reporter means having good sources, Schmidt is a very good reporter. But he is not a Republican and he was not on the Select Committee. *The New York Times* wrote far more stories about Secretary Clinton's email arrangement with herself than our committee had hearings on that same topic.

We had only one public hearing that even *remotely* touched upon her emails. One. One public hearing versus more than a hundred private interviews with witnesses about what happened before, during, and after the attacks.

In many respects, Benghazi was a murder investigation and I had plenty of experience with those. Shame on me for not being smart enough to know this was nothing like a courtroom: it was politics, and it was my fault for not seeing that sooner.

I did not correctly align expectations with what was reasonably likely or even with what was reasonably possible. My expectation—my idea of what success would look like—was simply to get some new answers; to discover new facts that the previous investigations had somehow missed. Those were not the expectations of most other observers of our committee's work. As the chairman, it was my responsibility to set the right expectations and to meet them. When your expectations are misaligned with others' expectations, that is a recipe for failure.

The jury I was trying to communicate to was not the jury anyone else was trying to communicate to. Ordinarily, the family and friends of those killed in a terrorist attack would be a more than sufficient jury. Add to that the men who survived the attacks at both the diplomatic facility and the Annex and you have the makings of a jury worth serving. But it was naïve of me to not realize that others would conclude the jury was broader and less personalized, especially in the modern political environment on the edge of a presidential race.

Secretary Clinton's public testimony was largely a failure in my judgment. A failure when it came to process and tacitly acknowledging artificial time limits that consistently worked against constructiveness. A failure in not understanding that the media, as a form of a jury, would demand that "new" information come from this hearing. Yes, I am aware of the irony of the media demanding "new" information from an investigation most in the media did not believe was necessary to begin with. A failure in that the investigation lasted way too long. A failure in realizing that even those disposed to be supportive of the Select Committee were primarily interested in questions about her emails as opposed to questions about security profiles in Libya.

One of my most vivid memories of Secretary Clinton's public hearing was looking into that full committee room and seeing Ty Woods's widow. She had been incredibly supportive throughout the investigation. Her singular interest in the investigation was simply knowing what happened, when it happened, why it happened, and as much as could be known about Ty's final hours.

More than seven years after Ty Woods was killed trying to protect his country and his friends, his widow, Dorothy, sent me a picture of their son. Seven years after Ty was killed. Three years after the Select Committee ended. One year after I left Congress. It was never about politics to her. Meeting her expectations is enough for me now and that should have been my own expectation from the beginning.

But this was not a homicide case, and no matter how often the names of the four men killed in service to our country were called, that hearing would be about the secretary of state. Could it have ever been successful? What were reasonable but still admirable expectations? It depends on what your objective was. I struggle to think of any recent congressional hearings that could safely be described as successful. But another famous one comes to mind that embodies failures similar to my own.

HOW MUELLER FELL SHORT

Robert Mueller was a marine, United States attorney, and director of the FBI. He had a solid reputation for integrity according to most Americans. Yet even he could not escape unscathed in the modern political environment. You can read his report for yourself and make up your own mind about that. It is the hearing I want to focus on as another example of mismatched expectations. As you might recall, Mueller spent two years investigating what Russia did to the United States during the 2016 election and with whom, if anyone, Russia conspired. And after his investigation was completed he issued a report. That should have been enough. Two years. Two volumes of material. Read it for yourself and draw your own conclusions. That's not too much to ask of us in a participatory democracy, is it?

But it was not enough for some, so Mueller was brought to Capitol Hill to testify. Think back if you can on what the expectations were for his appearance. As I recall, the expectations were very high in some circles. Some argued that Mueller would breathe "new life" into an investigation that had been going on for over two years. That would be hard to accomplish. Others argued that Mueller would bring his report to vivid life. Think about that for a second. He spent two years interviewing hundreds of witnesses and examining thousands of pieces of evidence. His office issued indictments, secured guilty pleas, and had full-fledged jury trials. And the expectation was that a member of Congress, in five minutes, could breathe new or vivid life into this investigation? Really?

What about Mueller and his expectations? You can begin with the fact that he did not want to appear. He made that crystal clear. Sometimes reluctant witnesses can make effective witnesses, but not when the full body of his or her work is already on full public display. What about the characteristics of the witness himself or herself? Would that meet expectations? Not if you have ever met or witnessed Bob Mueller testify before. He is precisely what you expect a former marine, former United States attorney, and former director of the FBI to be: fact centric, measured, and clinical.

So, you had a reluctant witness who had already written reams on what he wanted to say, was limited in other respects by the strictures of the grand jury process and the classification of certain evidence, had a well-earned reputation for being cautious and measured, and *that* was supposed to make for dramatic television?

Republicans are often guilty of setting unrealistically high expectations for public congressional hearings, but some of that lack of realism is rooted in the increasingly strong headwind the DC media creates for Republicans.

What did we learn today that we did not already know?

What is new?

Hasn't this ground been covered before?

Those are the questions we frequently got from the folks at *Politico, The Hill, The New York Times,* and *The Washington Post.* And when I say "frequently," I mean like every, single time.

The headwind is different for Democrats, or at least it was when I was there. By "different" I mean there is no headwind at all. And yet the Mueller hearing was still a flop. A flop like the Clinton hearing. A flop like the Strzok public hearing. A flop like almost every other congressional hearing you can think of.

That is what happens when you set expectations that can never be met and try to meet those expectations in an investigative structure as fundamentally flawed as the current congressional investigative structure.

The Mueller hearings proved these same points yet again. Prosecutors, like Mueller, do not usually make compelling witnesses period, and especially not in five-minute increments. Think about it logically: The written report required two years to compile. How could you possibly distill it in five-minute increments simply by responding to other people's questions? You really could not devise a scheme less calculated to succeed than that. If something new *had* come up in the hearing, what would your likely response have been? *Well, how in the hell did you miss that during the two years you spent investigating? You must be a lousy investigator if you failed to find a significant fact in two years with a multimillion-dollar budget and a team of FBI agents if a member of Congress found it in five minutes!* There was never going to be new information found by Congress that a lengthy investigation did not already find.

So, the hearings—at both the Judiciary Committee and the Intelligence Committee—were persuasive failures. I daresay you would struggle to find a single person who changed his or her mind based on Mueller's public testimony.

If the jury has already made up its mind, and the mechanisms of persuasion available to you include responding to questions in five-minute increments, and expectations have been set ridiculously high for your testimony, that is a recipe for failure.

That is not to say that Mueller himself is a failure. He is not, nor does it necessarily impact the investigative work done throughout the process. I daresay many of those expressing opinions on the Benghazi investigation and Mueller's investigation did not fully read either report issued. Minds were principally made up over media reporting and the public hearings.

And people disproportionately remember how things end, as opposed to the beginning or the fulsomeness of the investigation itself, and the ending was a tortured duet of hearings where persuasion gave way to sheer ratification and validation of previously held beliefs. Even by that standard, both of the hearings were failures in my judgment.

Persuasion requires symmetry. There must be symmetry between the expectations of those involved. There must be symmetry in the manner and form in which we are communicating. There must be a willingness to both move and be moved by the convictions of others—rooted, of course, in fact and authenticity.

The persuasive failures I have suffered as a prosecutor, congressman, family member, or friend have largely been grounded in misaligned expectations. These failures have also occurred because I either failed to recognize or flat out rejected the obvious jury, did not carefully calibrate a realistic objective, or failed to gauge the burden of proof necessary to further the goal.

Learn from me and my mistakes. Remember these things. Don't get greedy. Set realistic expectations and be sure to align them with your bigger purpose, objective, and goal. And most important, take your small wins. It is far better to set low expectations and exceed them than to fail to meet higher expectations. I still cringe when I see cops, prosecutors, or members of the House or Senate set high expectations. "Someone will be indicted!" "Someone is going to go to prison!" "We're going to shock the world!" "This is treason!" Those are all very lofty expectations. If you are going to overachieve, overachieve with the delivery, not the expectations. Under-promise and overperform.

There are precious few Perry Mason moments in life where you get a defendant to confess on the witness stand, where you get a political opponent to concede that your healthcare plan is better than his or hers, where your teenage child screams, "Yes! I will immediately begin to study more because I want to reach my fullest potential and ascend to the top ranking in my middle school class!" Life does not happen that way, and if you think communications success happens that way, you will be wildly disappointed.

Persuasion is incremental. It is subtle. It is sometimes indiscernible. Human nature does not like to concede error. We are better at rationalization than we are at confession. Getting someone to reconsider a position is persuasive success. Getting someone to listen without prejudice to your position is persuasive success. Getting someone to understand where you are coming from is persuasive success.

The best way to avoid failure—external or internal—is to set the right expectations. If you accept that those moments of complete transformation are rare, then what is a realistic goal? Think commonality. Think movement. Think progress. Think subtle shifts over time.

Moses never got to set foot in the Promised Land. He saw it but never experienced it. Martin Luther King, Jr., was murdered before he had a chance to see Barack Obama sworn in as president, Tim Scott take a seat in the U.S. Senate, or Condoleezza Rice serve in the highest echelons of government. You may never see the full fruits of your persuasion. You may be the first one in a long list of people who shift someone from one position to another. To that extent persuasion requires a certain humility, a willingness to start the work without finishing the work. You may never hear the words "You win! You got me! I finally see the light!" But it is Moses we remember more than Aaron. Taking someone to the edge of newness can sometimes be more historic than setting the first foot in it.

CHAPTER 16

HOW DO YOU KNOW IF YOU'VE GOT IT?

PAIN RELIEF

My father drives slowly. As in *painfully* slowly. As in when he is in the driver's seat, you might not be moving at all.

But on one particular day in May 2000, as he drove my wife and me to a debate, he could not drive slowly enough for me. I wanted to catch every stoplight. I prayed the train would come and that it would malfunction and stop on the tracks, blocking the road out of our neighborhood. I prayed for a flat tire. A blown engine. A meteorite. The Second Coming.

That February, I left the U.S. Attorney's Office to run for circuit solicitor in my hometown of Spartanburg. You cannot run for partisan, political office as an assistant U.S. attorney, so I had no choice but to resign as a federal prosecutor. A circuit solicitor is what the rest of the country calls a district attorney. He or she is the chief prosecutor of state crimes for a region or jurisdiction. Different states have different ways of determining who the district attorney is and how that district attorney is selected. In South Carolina, we elect our circuit solicitors for four-year terms and in the Seventh Judicial Circuit, the juris-diction consists of Spartanburg and Cherokee counties.

The incumbent circuit solicitor was a well-regarded pros-ecutor who had served as a prosecutor for more than two de-cades. I was challenging him in the Republican primary. In hindsight it was not a very smart thing to do on several levels: (1) Running for an elective office with an election in June and beginning the campaign in February is not a long time to pre-pare or campaign; (2) while I had prosecutorial experience, I had no state court prosecutorial experience before I ran for this office (federal court, yes, but not state court, and this was a state prosecutor race); and (3) running against any incumbent is mis-erable.

Cherokee County is home to many wonderful people and has a well-known landmark of a peach water tower. If you are a *House of Cards* fan, Frank Underwood was the congressman from Cherokee County, and there is a famous scene involving the peach water tower. Spartanburg County is home to my wife and me and is an incredible community with wonderful col-leges and universities and kind people. I was excited at the pros-pect of potentially serving these two counties. I was *not* excited to go head-to-head against the counties' beloved incumbent that day of the debate. (I guess I should give my dad some credit since I did get to the debate in time, with minutes to spare de-spite my desperate pleading to the heavens.)

I was *not* a person who had mastered the art of communica-tion and persuasion. I was not a person who had "got it."

A couple of decades later and things are very different now. I hate introductions when I speak, not because I am modest, but because whoever is introducing me is standing between me and my desire to communicate with and persuade those in at-tendance. I pray for green lights, no police, and a parking spot right next to the front door. I can't wait for the debate or speech to start.

Something happened along the way, and the young man who was terrified of a public debate figured out how to love the art of persuasion.

It happened in the courtroom too. Before any trial begins, the jury has to be assembled. The court then gives some introductory instructions to the jurors on the importance of paying close attention, the necessity of keeping an open mind and not consulting any outside sources, and the absolute requirement that no deliberating or discussing of the case take place before the last witness has testified and the last exhibit has been introduced. Those introductory comments take about twenty minutes. During my first ten jury trials I wanted these opening remarks to last forever. I wanted the judge to start with the "Magna Carta" and work his way forward. I wanted a full history on the right to trial by jury, the reason we have twelve jurors and not nine or fifteen, the history of who sits where in a courtroom and why. As the judge began to get closer and closer to the end of his pretrial instructions, I could feel my heart begin to beat faster, my breathing become quicker, and my general sense of anxiety take over. I was nervous. I dreaded what was about to happen.

And then that something happened.

Somewhere between trial ten and trial fifteen, I could feel not my heart beating faster, but my leg moving up and down. I was ready for those pretrial instructions to end because the judge was the only thing between me and the jury. I cannot pinpoint precisely why it changed or the precise moment that it did, but a change had taken place, and the nervous young prosecutor could not wait until it was his turn to talk.

I remember my first live television interview once I got to

Congress. I was being interviewed by Megyn Kelly from the Cannon House Office Building rotunda. I stared at the tops of my shoes during the entire interview. Literally. It is cringeworthy now, and it is a miracle any host ever asked me to come back on. But I was nervous. It was live television, there was no safety net, and I am sure Ms. Kelly wondered who booked this idiot on her show.

Successful litigators, public speakers, television guests, and communicators in general are not born. There is a painful growth process. Eventually that pain goes away and peace is left. A peace that comes from being prepared and knowing the objective you seek to accomplish. That Pasteur quote that makes my children's eyes roll is true: Chance *does* favor the prepared mind. Success always rewards a healthy sense of both self-confidence and self-awareness. If you are not a funny person, it makes little sense to begin your interactions with a joke. If you are by nature a serious person, find something serious as a theme to run through what you are communicating. Knowing the facts is essential to effective communication. But so too is knowing yourself. And giving yourself a chance to grow into the communicator you aspire to be.

PRACTICE MAKES PERSUASION

When I hired young litigators at the solicitor's office, they needed two things: confidence and practice. We didn't start in the courtroom. We started in the conference room. I would have them stand up and convince me to go see their favorite movie. That was the challenge—convince me that your favorite movie is worth my time.

The jury is easy: It's just one person who happens to like a good movie.

The objective is easy: Convince me to go see a movie.

The burden of proof is low: You aren't trying to get me to loan you $10,000, just to go see a movie.

It's not combative: I invited you to persuade me. I am a willing listener.

Some did well. Many did not. These were lawyers who spent three years in law school. More than that, they had expressed an interest in standing in front of twelve people, not one, and convincing those twelve to do something far more significant than give a movie recommendation.

The good news is that almost every one of them got better with time, with practice, and with understanding the means and purpose of effective persuasion.

The mistakes I made early in my career were many and largely rooted in two areas: not understanding the dynamics of persuasion and not understanding the nature and characteristics of those I was seeking to persuade.

Understand Fully What You Are Doing.

One of the most divisive topics in our culture is the issue of life—when it begins, who decides when it begins, and the role the state or federal government should have in defining, implementing, or restricting those beliefs. It is one of those issues on which nearly everyone has an opinion but most do not want to discuss it.

It was for all of those reasons and more that I was initially reluctant to talk about these issues when asked to address groups or give speeches.

I spent a rainy Sunday afternoon in my home office in Spartanburg having a long discussion with myself about what precisely I did believe, why I believed it, and how I could communicate it to a broader audience.

What emerged was a speech about life that does not mention the word "abortion" a single time.

What emerged was a speech about life that does not mention the word "trimester" a single time.

What emerged was a speech about life that focuses on the lives in the room. How did the people sitting in that room value their own life? In what ways did they assign worth to their own existence?

What emerged was a way to communicate at the margins in a way that hopefully compels the listener to think about the issue differently and resolve ambiguities or close calls in the favor of the positions I hold.

You can be subtle and powerful. You can be measured and accomplish your objective. You can live at the margins and still have your persuasion reach the heart of the matter. In fact, I believe that is where the best chance of the longest-lasting persuasion exists. The real, significant change will occur when the listener makes up his or her own mind, drawing the final logical line himself or herself.

I rarely asked someone to vote for me in any of the races I ever ran in. Of course, I wanted them to. The political "experts" who managed campaigns insisted it was needed, and I am sure I succumbed to their advice in campaign ads or literature. But it was too obvious to me. Who runs for office without wanting people to vote for him or her? Make your case and then let the voter fill in the remaining step, which is the vote.

I do not recall ever asking a jury to convict a defendant in opening statement. How could you ask them to? The jury had not heard from a single witness or examined a single piece of evidence. Why would you risk your credibility by asking a juror to "convict" someone literally before the trial even officially began? What would they base that conviction on? The fact that a person had been charged? Indicted? Was on the opposite side of the courtroom?

That analysis runs completely counter to what the judge had just admonished them, which was that the defendant was presumed innocent until proven guilty. And, quite frankly, you run the risk of alienating the jury by doing the one thing they had just agreed they would not do: make up their minds before the trial was over.

So, I am a prosecutor who didn't like to ask for convictions and a politician who didn't like to ask for votes, yet I had pretty good runs of success at both. Trust me and my experience—there is another way. There is a role for subtlety in persuasion. There is a place for letting the jury draw the last connecting dot. There is a way to convince the jury to do what you think is right, just, and fair based on the evidence and testimony and at the right stage of the trial.

Understand Human Nature.

You might recall that Dr. Kevin Gilliland is the reason I took more psychology classes than any other discipline in college and that Judge Ross Anderson is the one who sent me on field trips to see that human nature on full, practical display. A desire to succeed as a communicator is what ultimately led me to converge the academic with the practical. This eventually led to a total obsession to know how a jury and audience think.

First, people do not listen in groups. They listen individually. It does not matter if you are talking to fifteen thousand people or five people. If you can do the latter, you can do the former, and the process is exactly the same. It is daunting to look at a sea of people from the speaker's podium. People have a real fear of public speaking and their fear is oftentimes in direct proportion to the size of the crowd. I get that. I just don't get *why*. When you are talking to a large group, remember that they are not listening as a large group. (Okay, sure, there are some herd mentality characteristics at play—for instance, people are more likely to clap if others are clapping, laugh if others are laughing, boo if others are booing.) But fundamentally people hear on an individual level.

There is no such thing as "public speaking" because there is no such thing as "public listening." People process information individually, they hear different things even if the words are exactly the same, and they reach conclusions based on their own experience, education, and bias. So, if we are not nervous talking to one person, why would be nervous talking to a hundred versions of that one same person?

Even members of Congress as good and talented as Representative Elise Stefanik have fears when it comes to speaking and live television. Elise is one of my favorite people in the world and, to me, she epitomizes all the right reasons to go into public service. I did not know her well until Speaker Ryan told me I would be joining the House Intelligence Committee and he noted, "Elise will wind up being one of your favorite colleagues." Kevin McCarthy told me the same thing. Both were right. I sat by her on the Intelligence Committee for two years and sat by her on the floor of the House during votes.

Before one of our hearings, which would be televised nationally, she commented that she was a little apprehensive to be staring into a sea of television cameras. "Treat it as one camera, Elise," was my suggestion. "It's one camera just like doing a normal television interview." Each of those hundred cameras will be capturing the same thing, so what is the difference in number if all of them are serving precisely the same function?

She said it helped her. Fast-forward nearly two years when she was back on national television during the House Intelligence Committee hearings on impeachment. I sent her a quick text of encouragement. "It's just one camera," was her response (with a smiley face)! People process information individually just as the camera captures you singularly. Do not be over-whelmed by size or volume.

Furthermore, most people are forgiving and will overlook (or flat out miss) mistakes. Every time I do a speech or an inter-view, I count the errors I made—wrong word, poor grammar, missed opportunity, failure to use the optimal timing, you name it. I am consistently, albeit pleasantly, surprised at how few of those mistakes were heard by the audience. That is, unless it is an important fact and they believe you were intentionally wrong. That, they will not overlook or mitigate! But almost all else they grade on the curve.

The dynamics of persuasion include those elements you have already learned: the jury, the objective, the burden of proof, and the calibration of that burden with the objective. You know your goal. You know your audience. You've got the tools. But what about the metrics for success? How do you judge and measure success when it comes to a love of and a proficiency in persuasion? How do you know when you have reached certain milestones? How do you know if you've got it?

You will know you are on your way to being a better com-municator when you don't pray for trains, red lights, and med-ical emergencies because you are too terrified to make a speech in public.

You will know you are making progress on your journey to effective communication and persuasion when the labored breathing and rapid heartbeat are replaced with that leg that won't stay still because it is almost your turn to go and you sim-ply cannot wait.

You will know you are closing in on your target of being a great communicator and persuader when you can get the result you want without even asking for it. You have done such a good job of using facts, expressing authenticity, calibrating your burden of proof, and employing the power of questions such that your objective is clear not only to you; it is clear to everyone listening to you.

You will know you have arrived when the contrary positions or beliefs of others no longer threaten or irritate you. They represent an opportunity, not a challenge. They represent an opening to discuss, not an invitation to argue.

Countless times during my weekly trip to the grocery store on Saturday mornings, well-intentioned people will ask some derivation of this question: "How do you keep from going crazy listening to all of that stuff in DC? How do you keep from pulling your hair out?"

The second question is easy: because I do not want to be bald. The first question is pretty easy too: because contrary positions, beliefs, or convictions do not offend me. They represent both an opportunity to learn and an opportunity to persuade. "Persuading" people who already agree with you is what is impossible. That's not persuasion. That's ratification and validation and frankly not much of a challenge. Persuading those who do not agree with you—even persuasion at the margins—is where the excitement and the challenge lie. And the most effective, longest-lasting form of persuasion is when you take the other person to the brink of change, incremental or otherwise, and watch as that person takes the final step.

Can you do that?

Can you finally *enjoy* the challenge that persuasion provides? Can you get to your destination by letting others take the final step?

DON'T EVEN ASK

Ruby Nell Lindsey was a loving, wonderful mother, daughter, friend, co-worker, and wife. Her husband, Marion, was neither loving nor wonderful. He physically assaulted Nell in front of their children. He attacked her on family vacation. He struck her in the face in the parking lot of an Applebee's restaurant. Marion Lindsey put alcohol in a baby's bottle for their youngest son. He referred to their oldest son using a sexual orientation epithet. He had a history of abuse and violence toward others. He was abusive, physically and verbally, toward Nell. He showed utter disregard and contempt for court orders and conditions of bond.

So, it was no surprise to anyone when Nell made the difficult, courageous decision to leave Marion Lindsey—no surprise to anyone except Marion Lindsey. A woman's decision to leave an abusive relationship often brings with it even more peril. I know that sounds counterintuitive—that leaving danger is dangerous—but it's true. The time immediately after a woman leaves an abusive relationship can often be the most perilous.

Marion Lindsey disabled Nell's car so she would not be able to travel back and forth to work at a local hospital, but Nell was resourceful. And she had a dear friend, Celeste Nesbitt, willing to help her.

On September 18, 2002, Celeste Nesbitt picked Nell up after work to drive her back to her home in Inman, South Carolina. Celeste was driving. Celeste's mother was in the front passenger seat. Nell was in the back seat on the driver's side. Celeste's young daughter was in a car seat in the middle of the back seat and Celeste's other young daughter was in the back seat on the passenger side. They were headed home after a hard day of work. It was night. It had been a long day. It had been a long month.

They recognized the car simultaneously, Nell and Celeste. It was Marion Lindsey following them. There was a court order in place directing Marion Lindsey to stay away from his wife, Nell, but Marion did not care. There was a bond condition directing Marion Lindsey to have no contact with his wife, but he did not care. Court orders and bond conditions were mere paper to Marion Lindsey, and mere paper could not stop him.

When Celeste Nesbitt recognized Marion Lindsey's car, she did a very smart thing. Rather than head home, she headed straight for the police department in Inman, South Carolina. She ran red lights, she ignored stop signs, and she crossed railroad tracks at triple the recommended speed. She was going to get Nell Lindsey to the protective clutches of law enforcement. She was going to get Nell to the police station. She was going to let law enforcement deal with Marion Lindsey so she and Nell did not have to. And she did. Almost.

Nell Lindsey was on the phone with 911 detailing Marion Lindsey's violent past and his real and present threat as Celeste pulled into the back parking lot of the Inman Police Station. And as she pulled into the parking lot, police officers came out the back door and Marion Lindsey pulled into the parking lot as well.

Marion got out of his car, went straight to the driver's side back seat with his weapon drawn, and fired four shots through the glass window. Nell Lindsey died with the cellphone in her hand, 911 on the line, and police officers mere feet away. The children in the back seat with Nell had climbed onto the floorboard. That saved their lives as at least one of the bullets from Marion Lindsey's gun struck the car seat a child had just gotten out of.

Marion Lindsey claims he then turned the gun on himself in an effort to take his own life. Again, it's strange how accurate shots killers are when it comes to shooting others but what poor, inaccurate shots killers are when it comes to shooting themselves. Marion Lindsey's bullets hit Nell Lindsey. Marion Lindsey's bullets missed Marion Lindsey.

Marion Lindsey was arrested and charged with the murder of Nell Lindsey. He would stand trial for his life since, in addition to murder, the shooting took place in a public place and endangered others.

Make your closing argument.

The guilt phase is over. Marion Lindsey was found guilty. The sentencing phase is almost over. All that is left is for you to address the jury one final time before the jury retires to deliberate and decides whether to sentence him to life or death.

The jury could not be clearer, it's the twelve people seated right in front of you.

The burden of proof is the highest the law recognizes, beyond a reasonable doubt.

The objective, well, that is a little more complicated. Is the objective to have him sentenced to death? Is the objective to be fair? I am at peace with the objectives I identify and pursue in capital cases, but you are the prosecutor now, so what is your objective?

The calibration between the objective and the burden of proof? That depends on which objective you identify, doesn't it?

What would you say, how would you say it, in what order would you sequence your closing argument? Would you start bold or get the perfunctory matters out of the way and slowly build to a crescendo?

I left for the courthouse at daybreak, hours before the jury was to report for closing argument. I pulled off in the parking lot of a church and sat in my truck for close to two hours having a conversation with myself about proportionality, second chances, mercy, and retribution, but mostly about justice: *What is the just result?* It was almost twenty years ago but I can remember the conversation with myself better than ones I had with myself last week. *What do I really believe? Why do I believe it? Can I structure the closing argument effectively? Can I make a closing argument in a death penalty case without ever asking the jury to put the defendant to death?*

That's what I walked into the courthouse and did. I made a closing argument in a death penalty case without that one, big, final request of the jury. My heart was calm because I knew what I believed. My leg was bouncing because I understood what I wanted to accomplish and I understood, if just for a moment, human nature: the humanity of Nell, the inhumanity of Marion, and the humanity of the jury.

The crime is clear. The consequences of what Marion Lindsey did will echo through eternity for Nell, her mother, her children, and those who loved her. The consequences of what Marion Lindsey did will forever be etched in the memories of those two little girls lying on the floorboard of their mother's car, listening to a woman beg for her life, hoping and praying the bullets don't end their lives as they did Nell's. And now it is time to determine what is the proper punishment for this man—for this crime.

At one end of the spectrum is mercy. We all need it. We have all benefited from it at some time or another in our lives. Mercy comes in many forms. It can come in the form of second chances, which this defendant had. It can come in the form of a new beginning, which this defendant had. It can come in the form of a wife who loved you, which this defendant had. It can come in the form of children, and the blessings attendant thereto, which this defendant had. This defendant tasted sweet mercy in life and it did not keep him from killing an innocent woman. It did not keep him from endangering the lives of innocent children. I do not, I cannot, I will not stand before you and ask you to show mercy to this man again. And for anyone who does stand before you and ask you for mercy—yet again—for this defendant, I want you to ask yourself: Why is it that those who ask for mercy most often are so incapable of ever showing it to others? Why do those who beg you for mercy never show it to others?

At the other end of the spectrum from mercy is vengeance. Retribution. An eye for an eye, a tooth for a tooth. I do not stand before you today to ask you for your vengeance. I am not asking you to take this man's life like he took Nell's. I am not asking you to deprive him of life's goodbyes, of the ability to put his affairs in order before he meets his judgment. I am not asking you to leave him slumped in the back seat of a car, deprived of his goodbyes, without a chance for a final prayer. I am not asking you to shoot him in the back parking lot of a building dedicated to justice, peace, and safety. I am not asking you to do to him what he did to Nell.

Each of us will die. It is not death that scares us. It is the manner in which that death visits us. Sometimes death walks slowly to the front door of our lives, we can see it coming, we can make amends with those we have offended, we can right any wrongs accumulated along the way, we can love those we have neglected, we can hold those we will miss the most, we can put our affairs in order, say our goodbyes, prepare our souls, and by the time that gentle knock comes on the front door of our lives we are ready. That is the death we aspire to.

That is not the death Nell Lindsey was given. Death

kicked in the front door of her life without a warning. One moment you are at work, dreaming of seeing your own children, the next moment you are driving for your life to the sanctuary of a police station, begging for your life on a 911 call with a stranger. It wasn't your own mother's voice that you last heard. It wasn't the angelic cadence of your own children; it was a stranger on a 911 call.

What would Nell Lindsey have given to have a jury like you decide her fate? What would Nell Lindsey have given to have you decide whether she lives or dies? What would Nell Lindsey have given to have a chance to plead for her life to reasonable, responsible people? No, I am not asking you to do to him what he did to her.

I do not, will not, cannot ask you to show mercy to someone who never showed it to others. But neither do I ask you to walk to the other side of the spectrum and give him the same sentence, in the same way, with the same depravity he gave Nell Lindsey.

I stand in the middle of mercy and vengeance. On a rock called Justice. And from this rock you can see the full panoply of this crime. I stand on a rock called Justice and from this rock you can see the havoc he wreaked on so many innocent lives. I stand on a rock called Justice and say that taking another's life does not always mean you forfeit your own, but sometimes it does. Sometimes it does. Sometimes it does.

There is a time when the circumstances of another's crime, the character of the defendant, and the impact of his deeds call out for the most severe form of lawful punishment we have. You are the collective conscience of this community. You decide what the proper punishment is. And we will respect whatever that decision may be. God give you wisdom as you render a verdict—that speaks the truth.

Sometimes your jury cannot answer you—not out loud at least. But they will answer you. They will answer you in the quietness of their own conscience and then, even more directly, when they render their verdict.

CHAPTER 17

MY CLOSING ARGUMENT

INNER PERSUASION

The church my family and I attend is a Baptist church in South Carolina. On certain occasions, you might expect patriotism to be mixed in with the preaching. Whether it is the Fourth of July, Memorial Day, the weekend before Election Day, or Veteran's Day, there is a mixture of military, love of country, and love of God.

I am not smart enough to unlock how love of God and love of country fit together within the teachings of Christ. However, this is not a theological exegesis. This is my closing argument to you, dear reader. This is my final attempt to convince you that the quizzical approach to life might work and how the best practice partner you will ever have as it relates to effective communication and persuasion is yourself, but only if you are honest within the candor of your own mind and ask the right questions.

One year around the Fourth of July, my wife and I were sitting in a service when the message began to steer toward our

Founding Fathers and how they were "inspired by God." I found myself just like I did in that little house on the eastside of Spartanburg many years ago. It's amazing how a well-lit church pew can become a pitch-black closet for the big questions to take shape.

What would I hear if I were a person of color in a sermon about the founding of our country? What would I hear if I were a woman listening to the founding of our country on "biblical" principles? What do I hear as a white person about the founding of our country? And how could those points be explored with questions, even if those questions were to myself?

Do you believe the Bible contains truths? Are those truths timeless or have they evolved over the course of our own evolution of the human condition? Has God changed His mind on moral issues? Can God even change His mind or, because He is God, did He realize where His mind would wind up regardless and therefore that represents no "change"?

If God is truth and those truths are timeless, does it follow that what is right today has always been right? If that is true, does it follow that what is wrong today has always been wrong? Yes, I am well aware that mankind can evolve, but you weren't arguing that the country was inspired by mankind at its inception. You were arguing that the foundation was inspired by God, weren't you? I thought that's what began this entire exchange.

Isn't it wrong for one man to own another? Can a man consent to be owned by another or is that one freedom you are not "free" to surrender? How would one even begin to consent to such a thing, or is it intrinsically noxious to even allow a free people, in theory, to consent to certain anti-freedoms?

Is it true that in Christ there is no Jew or Gentile, no rich or poor, no male or female? Would it also be true that there is no black, brown, or white? No slave, no owner? How can one believer not value as equal another believer?

Was it ever "right" for a human being to be considered— legally or otherwise—less than a full human being? Do I understand that certain "compromises" were included in our foundational document? Yes, but I didn't hear you argue that the document was inspired by "compromise." I thought you were arguing that it was "inspired by God." Do you think God approved of the three-fifths compromise?

If there is no male or female in Christ, could there be a male and a female in a document inspired by Him?

I have my own beliefs, as I am sure you do too. How frequently do you challenge your own beliefs? How often do you run your belief structure through your own series of logical, factual, spiritual, or moral calisthenics?

I do it all the time, unfortunately. (I say "unfortunately" because it can be really exhausting!) Some would argue that it is a sign of weakness to be in a constant state of evaluation. Obviously, I disagree. I think you would want to be strong enough in your convictions to make sure you know exactly what you believe, why you believe it, and what, if anything, could amend even in the slightest, that belief structure.

I believe you can and should have these conversations with yourself.

On the issue of what women and men of color might hear in a July Fourth church service, my motivation was not to be better able to argue but rather to be better able to understand. My motivation was the two friends who came into my mind sitting in that church service: Tim Scott and Sheria Clarke.

If I want to understand Tim's involvement with law enforcement or the challenges of being a conservative of color in American politics, the least I can do is anticipate what questions he might have. I have never been black a day in my life, but that should not keep me from trying to understand the questions he would have. I have certainly never been a female of color like Sheria Clarke. I would doubly have no idea what it is like to be a young woman trying to live a faith-centric life in Washington. And I would have absolutely no idea what thoughts would go through a young black, conservative woman's mind. But I can try. I can do the best I can to anticipate and even, within all of my limitations, try to ask the questions she would ask. It is a double blessing if you can pull it off: Your mind will expand and you will develop compassion and understanding for people who have experienced things you will never experience.

It is the desire to listen, learn, and anticipate that will also propel you to choose your words carefully when you are interacting in sensitive areas where emotions and experience drive different perspectives.

It is oftentimes enough, when discussing issues with others, to simply say, "I am open to being persuaded." In fact, I end many comments with my family, friends, and co-workers by stating my observations and then concluding with this offer: "But I am open to being convinced I am wrong."

It is not only persuasive in its disarming authenticity—it is a gift you can give yourself: the open-mindedness of being persuadable.

I was doing a question-and-answer session with some attendees of a function in Texas recently and in response to one of their questions, I said: "This is what I believe but I am open to being convinced I am wrong." One of the attendees took offense. He likened the open-mindedness to being persuaded with a lack of conviction. "Surely there are some things for which you would never change your mind?"

There are countless issues where I have analyzed all I know to analyze and assumed all I know to assume and worked my way through the full body of evidence, and I am firmly convinced in a position. That is true. The question is: Are you open to something you have not already thought of? Are you open to the possibility that a new fact will emerge? Are you open to the discovery of never-before-discovered evidence and facts?

I think we have to be, don't we? Don't we have to be willing to do what we are asking others to do, which is to be persuadable?

Internally we should keep a running dialogue with ourselves. To avoid frightening others, that inner dialogue is probably best kept silent. If you cannot accomplish that (and I have certainly failed at that before), put your earbuds in and walk around so at least people think you might be on the phone rather than having an open and audible conversation with yourself.

THE IMPRESSIVE SIDE

Former Spartanburg mayor Bill Barnet became the mayor of the city of Spartanburg because he was written in by the voters of Spartanburg. That's right! He didn't run. He was drafted, won as a write-in, and, after two terms as mayor, left office at the peak of his popularity.

He was someone I relied on and whose opinion I valued greatly. I still do, even though neither of us is in government anymore. He was tepid at best on my run for Congress in 2010. It had nothing to do with electoral success prospects. It had everything to do with how you spend the most fleeting of all resources: your time.

"You will spend half of your life on airplanes and the other half in airports," was his pretty-accurate assessment of Congress. "All to be just one 1 of 435 members."

He was right about how my time would be spent. Most members do not live in Washington and that is for a variety of reasons, ranging from economics to local politics (and no, having members live in Washington would not alone heal the political divide in our country).

I had weekly flights to Washington, DC, for eight years, but I had it easy. Imagine Rep. Tulsi Gabbard's commute from Hawaii, or Senator Steve Daines's commute from Montana, or Minority Leader Kevin McCarthy's commute from California.

Thank the Lord for Wi-Fi on planes. And aisle seats. And earbuds. And occasional upgrades when no one is looking.

But on the descent into Washington Reagan National, the Wi-Fi stops working and you are alone with your thoughts. More often than not, the flight plan took us up the river with the city of Washington, DC, in full view on one side of the plane.

You get the overwhelming sense of inadequacy. You are flying into an airport named for Ronald Reagan and into a city named for George Washington. Every building is seemingly named after someone famous. There are monuments or memorials to George Washington, Thomas Jefferson, James Madison, Abraham Lincoln, and Martin Luther King, Jr. Every street name has significance. You feel so small and inconsequential. And that's even before you actually land and head toward Capitol Hill.

So much history. So much precedent. There is this sense that you cannot accomplish much, so you must therefore push, cajole, and expect others to do so. *Let the famous people do it,* was what I used to think. Let Speaker John Boehner do it or Speaker Paul Ryan after him. Let the Senate Majority Leader do it. Let the Supreme Court do it. Let those brave souls willing to run at the highest level do it. Surely 1 out of 435 members of Congress cannot accomplish much, if anything.

Congress is the butt of many a joke and the object of much derision. If only this team or that retook the majority. If only so-and-so would become chairman of this committee or that committee. If only this party or the other would do these things, the world would be a better place.

If only the president, regardless of who he or she is, would do something by executive fiat, or hold a press conference and extol the virtues of this policy or that policy; if only someone else would do something else, the world would be better place.

If only the Supreme Court would rule thusly, our culture would be better. If only the Supreme Court would unravel some intractable issue that has been perplexing this experiment in self-governance, the country would emerge from this malaise and thrive again.

We spend lots of time waiting on other people to do what it is we think should be done. We spend lots of time waiting on someone else to do the persuading, to do the communicating, to effectuate the change we want to see take place.

Part of that projection—that pushing of the responsibility to communicate change—is positional, isn't it? We expect political leaders to lead. We expect Supreme Court justices to rule or opine us toward social or cultural change. We expect others to do what we expect them to do. It has to be someone else's responsibility—after all, they are the ones who ran for office, they are the ones who raised their hands and said "Pick me." It has to be their responsibility. It has to be up to them. Universally, we expect them to do that.

But I do not.

I do not have higher expectations for those "leaders" than I do for you and that is true for many reasons.

Politics is a lagging indicator. Politics reflects rather than leads. That is not an indictment of those in public service, it's simply true. In fact, it's easily argued that reflection is precisely what the founders of our country really wanted on that Fourth of July centuries ago: They wanted the body politic to reflect the populace. Political races are not about persuasion anymore. When is the last time during a presidential political debate that you really got the sense a candidate was trying to use the tools of persuasion to prove to you there is a better way? Politics today is about ratification and validation rather than persuasion.

Waiting for the change you want to see reflected in the halls of Congress means someone else has already done the heavy lifting of persuading somewhere outside of Washington and the effect is finally beginning to be felt.

I do not believe it is someone else's job to do my job. If I believe strongly, passionately, and logically about an issue, why is it not also my responsibility to advocate for the change I want others to effectuate? Why would I wait for anyone else to do it?

Which is why the person we should begin to persuade first and foremost is ourselves. That might be the greatest job of communication you ever accomplish. Persuade yourself that you too have an obligation to join the discussion, join the debate, and engage in the conversation. Do so after you have marshaled the facts. Do so after you have considered every angle you can possibly discern. Do so consistent with the principles of effective advocacy we have studied during this book. But eventually you must do so.

IN WORD AND DEED

Think back on the course of your own life. When have you been moved to change? When have you been motivated to act? Who inspired you? Why were you inspired? What are those inflection points when you felt passionately about something and decided you would pursue it, even without any assurance of victory? What is your Thermopylae—the battle you are willing to wage even if victory is not guaranteed? Where is the battle you feel so strongly about that you will wage it even if defeat is guaranteed? What would you die for? What would you live for? What is your internal Melian dialogue—that conversation within yourself about those things you exist to do and to be?

Socrates was perhaps the greatest asker of questions that ever lived. He lost his life in part because of his quizzical nature. He is most famous for asking questions for which there was and remains no easy answer. It was not the destination he was consumed with. It was the process. He believed in the freedom to ask questions so much, he died for it.

Jesus knew the answer to every question He asked before He asked it, save perhaps one. He too lost His life in pursuit of something He was committed to. He asked questions of God, the religious and political leaders of His day, but the questions He asked of us are the ones that have stood the test of time and history and still serve as a guide for how we are to treat one another.

Martin Luther King, Jr., changed the world with no access to a library, no access to the Internet, just a pencil and some scraps of paper in a jail cell, alone, with his questions, his constant search to make us individually and collectively better, and willingness to ask no more of us than he was willing to do himself. He too died for what he believed.

Dietrich Bonhoeffer was a brilliant theologian, who risked and ultimately lost his life defending the right of other religious groups to simply exist, to live, to avoid being exterminated.

Some would argue democracy was preserved at that place called Thermopylae in a battle where the soldiers preserving democracy all died.

Heroes die like the rest of us. They just don't live like the rest of us. They find a purpose bigger than themselves, they pursue that purpose without regard to consequences, and therefore they do what it is we all strive to do: live a life that is persuasive enough to stand the test of time and the scrutiny of history.

I do not care what your beliefs are on any particular issue. If the circumstances of life have us in the same place, at the same time, and in the mood to discuss, perhaps we can try to out-persuade one another using questions and our rhetorical skill. Until then, do not wait on me and I will not wait on you. Equip yourself, arm yourself with facts and knowledge, allow yourself to be persuaded by better facts and better arguments, and then go be the change you wish someone would effectuate.

Know what you believe, why you believe it, be able to both defend it and understand why others believe differently, and then—in word and deed—persuade others.

THE PERSUASIVE SIDE

Mayor Barnet was right about what to expect in Congress—mainly the nagging sense of lost time trying to get from one place to another and then back again. There is not much to show for those eight years except a renewed sense of enlighten-ment on how to live what remains of this life.

There are two sides to every plane much like there are at least two sides to every issue. There is the side I peered out of in inadequacy and unworthiness—the side of the famous, the names we knew (or should have learned) in history class. That is the side we are tempted to look out of and wait on someone else to do our own job of persuasion. That is the easy side of the plane.

And there is the other side—the side that makes you feel even smaller but only because it took you so long to turn in that direction. That side of the plane where you see those ever so gently rolling green hills punctuated by elegant white crosses.

That side of the plane we call Arlington. Tragic, beautiful Arlington.

Where women and men with so many hopes, dreams, and boundless potential put everything on hold—even life—to serve something bigger than they were. Most of us would struggle to name anyone laid to rest at Arlington. Yet, most of us would agree it is that side of the plane that really founded this country—the side that fought to improve, uphold, and further the ideals our country aspires to.

Young, everyday men and women who found something worth serving and sacrificing for. That is the most persuasive side of the plane. That is the side of the plane that communicates to me the most.

You have the tools now. You know the mechanics of persuasion. You know how to use questions offensively and defensively. You know the power of logic and fact. You know how vital it is to identify the real jury and tailor your arguments toward them. You know there are no born communicators—that even the best were lousy at some point. They just refused to stay lousy.

Now, you just need a sense of obligation to go with your new skills and your plan. You need a reason to say *Why not me? Why shouldn't I be the one?*

Go be that which you want others to be. Go communicate what you believe and why you believe it in the most persuasive way possible. Be something worthy of reflection. Persuasion is hard. Everything in life worth doing is hard. But you too can be part of making sure this—the greatest experiment in self-governance the world has ever known—continues to refine herself into something continuously worthy of the sacrifice and service others made to get us this far.

ACKNOWLEDGMENTS

Terri, you are the kindest, sweetest, most beautiful, humble, and Christ-like person I have ever known. You have mastered the art of persuasion by doing the single most persuasive thing any of us can ever do, which is lead an authentic life wholly dedicated to the principles and precepts you believe in. I have never won an argument with or successfully cross-examined an authentically lived life. So, thank you, Terri, for making sure my cynicism always loses out to your hopefulness.

Watson and Abigail, it is not easy growing up the child of a prosecutor or a politician (or with a perfect mother). But you both carved your own path in life, succeeded academically in ways your father never did, and are caring, thoughtful, and considerate young adults. I could not be prouder of you.

Mom and Dad, thank you for valuing education and hard work and providing more for your children than either of you had growing up. Thank you, Dad, for making me read the dictionary and encyclopedia and limiting our television viewing such that I could not participate in any conversations at school about any popular shows. Mom, thank you for loving me no matter what I did or did not do.

Writing a book about persuasion, communication, and the art of asking the right questions requires a life made complete by both the questions asked and the answers provided by others. I have had so many incredible family members, friends, and co-workers through the course of life.

I am grateful to my three sisters, Laura, Caroline, and Elizabeth. I thought I wanted a brother, until I had three sisters. I would not change a thing.

Thank you to Cindy Crick, Missy House, Mary-Langston Willis, and Sheria Clarke (and your husbands and families) for sticking with me these many years. You could have and probably should have left for greener pastures many times. But you didn't. You stuck with a co-worker who embodies the two hardest qualities to abide: a total introvert who is addicted to golf. God is good when you get to live with Terri and work with y'all.

I am grateful to the women and men at the U.S. Attorney's Office—especially Beattie B. Ashmore, the Seventh Circuit Solicitor's Office, and the current circuit solicitor, Barry J. Barnette. Thank you to all the women and men who prosecuted cases at the United States attorney's office and the solicitor's office. That blindfolded woman is an exacting boss but you will never have one you can be prouder of.

As you will see reading this book, most members of Congress get along with one another most of the time. You will see some of my favorite colleagues, from both sides of the aisle, scattered among the pages of this book, but I want to say a special thank-you to Tim Scott (who persistently encouraged me to write this book), Johnny Ratcliffe, and Kevin McCarthy. When people ask me if I miss Congress, you are the reason the answer is "yes." I miss our dinners and the beautiful memories of our time fellowshipping together.

Thank you to the families who trusted me to prosecute cases involving their loved ones. There is a bond forged in pain and loss that transcends time and tenure in office.

Thank you to the women and men in law enforcement for giving me what I always wanted: a job I could be proud of at the end of life.

Thank you to the women and men who worked in our congressional offices in South Carolina and Washington. Public service can be noble and you epitomize that. As I said to you countless times, never confuse public disdain for Congress with yourselves. Everywhere I went in South Carolina there was a story of how you helped someone and those stories have nothing to do with political orthodoxies. Thank you to my current co-workers at Nelson Mullins.

Thank you to my friends, many of whom I have had for decades and decades, for the depth, breadth, and texture you added to life. Ben, Ed, Kevin, Robert, Keith, and so many others for being the brothers I didn't have.

Thank you to Esther Fedorkevich for making me do this.

Thank you to Lauren Hall for holding my hand and not letting me give up or switch to a screenplay for *True Detective Part IV*—and for not killing me when I know you thought about it.

Last, thank you to Mary Reynics and the entire Crown Forum team for giving me a chance to write about what I really wanted to write about and not what others might have expected me to write about.

ABOUT THE AUTHOR

TREY GOWDY is a former state and federal prosecutor who experienced the criminal justice system firsthand for nearly two decades. In 2010, he was elected to Congress and was chair of the House Committee on Oversight and Government Reform and chaired the Select Committee on Benghazi. He served on the House Permanent Select Committee on Intelligence, as well as the Judiciary, the Ethics, and the Education and Workforce committees. After four terms, he decided to not seek reelection, thus ending his career with an exemplary record in the courtroom and undefeated in political races. He has been widely recognized by law enforcement and victims of crime for his diligent service as a prosecutor and was chairman of the South Commission on Prosecution Coordination. He is the co-author of the *New York Times* bestseller *Unified*.

treygowdy.com
Facebook: @RepTreyGowdy
Twitter: @TGowdySC
Instagram: @tgowdysc

ABOUT THE TYPE

This book was set in Bembo, a typeface based on an old-style Roman face that was used for Cardinal Pietro Bembo's tract *De Aetna* in 1495. Bembo was cut by Francesco Griffo (1450–1518) in the early sixteenth century for Italian Renaissance printer and publisher Aldus Manutius (1449–1515). The Lanston Monotype Company of Philadelphia brought the well-proportioned letterforms of Bembo to the United States in the 1930s.